Evel Meckarov

The Journey

To

Self Mastery

CONTENTS

wholeheartedly give

Top Performance 100

I couldn't find the sports car of my dreams, so I built it myself. –
Ferdinand Porsche

Perception is Golden 104

It's not what we don't know that surprises us the most but what
we thought we knew

Success 109

Success is in the eye of the beholder

Financial Death By A Thousand Cuts 113

Sometimes, the best deals are those you don't make! – 45th US
President

Deals – Leverage Is Everything 120

Love may influence hearts and minds, but it is leverage that
permanently changes them

Teaching – A Two Way Street 128

If you want to perfect something, teach it. If you want to
understand people perfectly, teach them

Awareness is Everything 133

Professionalism without awareness is foolishness. It won't do you

any good to be the best violin player on the Titanic

INTRODUCTION

My name is <u>Evel Meckarov</u>. A professional PMP certified Senior Project/Program and Portfolio Manager with IBM as well as a Senior IBM certified master educator having taught hundreds of workshops to over 3000 people over the years.

One of the most powerful tools I have discovered in my life is the power of self-reflection. By self-reflecting on certain aspects of my professional and personal life during certain times since 2012 I have gained much needed clarity and understanding on the many areas of our modern age that present a challenge to most people I have met.

Over the years people on my workshops, appreciating the content, would ask me why I haven't written a book on some of the topics I have taught. My answer has always been that books are a dying medium and that in today's world of instant gratification, social media and online video very few would actually read it unless it was heavily promoted and heavily invested in with no profit in sight.

So, what has changed?

In February 2019 my daughter Amelia was born. I had realized my professional and personal life had been stable and happy for several years until then filled with meaning and fulfilling relationships, meaning my gained insights were bearing fruits and the time had come to share them as 'field tested' at least with the heirs of my kingdom. My plan is to teach my daughter, and any future children I may have, traditional values with patience and hard work.

This book is dedicated and written for them so that when the time is right, they have some guiding principles to help them along their journey.

Using my skills of a master educator, I have compiled those insights into concise and powerful chapters with a clear action plan you can take shall you wish to improve those aspects of your professional and personal life as well.

I invite you to share the journey with me on the following pages.

PERSONAL TRANSFORMATION

For the cherry blossoms to bloom, first the leaves must fall, and winter must take its toll

I've seen many people over the years longing for change, dreaming for that one big break, or even worse that prince or princess that will take their sorrows away and bring harmony and bliss. I've seen the same people years later, still lost in their dreams with almost no change in their life for the better or worse. I've often asked myself what went wrong for them, why are they still in the same place where they have always been despite their strong desire for something better?

The answer was more forthcoming than I expected. So simple yet so difficult to accept. For a lasting change in our lives that brings us closer to our dreams and visions of a grand future we must let go of the things, people and patterns that hold us back from those dreams. The past can't co-exist together with the future. If you wish to have any notable success, happiness and balance in today's world defined by change, you need to master the art of changing yourself first and letting go of everything that no longer serves your purpose.

I as well used to have those dreams of that one big break that would change my whole life forever. I spent most of my university years dreaming of that great life I would get someplace over the seas in the USA or Australia. Reality however, had something else to say and I am glad it did as I love the place I am currently at. Back in 2008 I had just suffered a big disappointment at work and the only way that I could think of fixing my disappointment, was to go back to the comforts of my past which was Macedonia.

While I spent a good year over there soul searching, finding myself and letting go of my past, the most powerful lesson that I brought back with me was: "Take the lessons of the past and let go of its emotions".

All of us at one point or another have had to let go of something from our past that no longer served our purpose and we know how difficult it has been. To make things worse, because of the strong emotional attachment we can even convince ourselves that our past is still necessary in our lives. How do we then get the courage and strength to get away from this trap?

Vision - Many people will tell you to be as specific as possible when creating your vision of the future but this is just another trap as many of those specifics will be influenced by your current limiting beliefs and will only hold you back further. Create a vision that strikes the right balance between specific goals and general directions.

Patterns - What are the patterns, beliefs and habits that are not bringing any value to you towards the realization of that vision? Try to be brutally honest with yourself as to why you are still stuck in these patterns? Is it only because of emotional attachments that you are not ready to break? Is it only for the comfort and false security they bring?

People - Once you create your vision and identify the patterns that you need to let go of; you will realize that certain people play a big part of those holding patterns as well. This is the sole reason most people fail to move forward. They are unable to emotionally let go of people in their life that hold them back. It is in many ways the most painful and difficult part of manifesting real and powerful change in our life. Sometimes these people can be partners, friends of many years or even members of family. This is not to say you need to break any contact or stop seeing them, but it is to say that you need to stop comparing your values to theirs or even worse trying to prove something to them or change their beliefs and life.

Patience - Real and lasting change does not happen overnight. Give yourself the proper time needed to reach emotional balance and a new balanced mindset after you have removed any major holding patterns or people from your life. Rushing to replace the old patterns with new ones while your emotions and new mindset are still not in balance will only cause you to attract different physical expressions and people of the same old patterns.

For the cherry blossoms to bloom first the leaves must fall and winter must take its toll. Lasting change is a process that has several phases. Something needs to die and a period of contemplation and balance is needed before a powerful future can realize its full potential and beauty.

There is no Holy Grail or magic red pill when it comes to change. The only thing that comes even close is the realization that the power to change yourself has always been within you and with it the power to change your future.

PURPOSE

Every once in a while, we find ourselves reflecting on the year that has gone by. Weighing the good and the bad, trying to make sense of it all and dreaming and setting goals for the year ahead. How can we take a dream, breath life into it and have it transform into something real that we can touch and see? No matter how good the year has been though, for the most of us, some goals and dreams were not reached and for some of us, this has been the case for several years in a row. How can we change that?

Let's try and solve our little mystery behind those major life goals that seem to be avoiding us like the plague letter year after year.

One of the most epic unrealized life goals is that set forth by a fellow called Cristoforo Colombo in the year of 1492. Cristoforo's life long goal had been to discover a trading route to India that at the time was only proposed in theory. He had been so convinced that his goal is attainable against all the odds and against all the better judgment of the royal navigators, that he had been willing to bet his life on it and be convincing and persistent enough to get the support from the

Queen of Spain Isabella of Castile herself.

Reading the history of great feats, we too often tend to focus only on the motives and goals behind the main protagonists, forgetting to realize that their voyages and lives were backed by powerful people in the background. Cristoforo would have never set a foot on a ship if his dreams would have not been aligned with the motives of other people and especially with those of the Queen.

Here-in may lie the greatest mystery of all the lost hopes and dreams: their lack of resonance with other people or a powerful sponsor. Half a millennium later this remains even more valid. In today's world where we are ever more inter-connected through the wonders of the exponentially growing digital sphere, the realization of any meaningful goal becomes almost impossible without the collaboration of many people. Even the goals we can buy ourselves into, mean we need to accomplish the goals of other people in order to make the money to allow us to do that.

Let's have a closer look at the art of giving life to our dreams by following few simple steps. Try not to think of what is possible and what is not. As is the case with Cristoforo, even if you set an impossible goal it may be just the one to lead you to places and situations you could never have hoped to imagine and evolving you to the point where you are ready to receive something even better than what you had originally set out to accomplish. A change of mindset is needed from the one of chasing dreams and goals to the one of becoming the right person to whom they come by themselves.

Purpose - Write down the three to five most important values you have as a person that make you wake up in the morning and make you believe your life has meaning and purpose. If there are more than five, try to be more general until you focus only on five. Is this: Quality of Life? Health? Love? Finance? Family? Friends? Spiritual Realization? Anything else that matters to you.

Dreams - What are the most important life dreams at this moment for you that are aligned with your core values and purpose? Each time you write down a dream of yours, it needs to be aligned with one of your three core values. If it is not, then you need to think twice of why you are wishing for this dream when your core values do not support it.

Goals - Now it is time to get down to earth a little bit and start breaking down each one of your dreams into specific, tangible real life goals that you can actually see and touch. Feel free to use S.M.A.R.T at this point of the process.

Sense - You have probably ended up with a huge wish list that makes you feel you have a higher chance of winning the lottery than ever bringing this list into your real life. Try to make sense of all these

18

goals and split them into several categories where they support each other or maybe even cancel each other out. Seeing how 5 seemingly non-related goals all work towards one single dream will increase your motivation and focus your energy towards what matters the most.

Actions - Once you have came up with the major groups of goals, it is time to think about the specific actions that are necessary in order to produce the results. Do not think at this stage about the cost of such actions. Cristoforo did not build those three ships that took him to America by himself.

Support - As a true manager, it is time to decide on who will actually perform all these actions. In some of the cases where personal goals are concerned, it will have to be you. Outsourcing your vacation to the Bahamas may not be the best idea. In most cases however, you will realize that those actions can be realized and supported by the combined effort of many other people or a single powerful sponsor.

Networks - Once you have identified the most ambitious actions in need of a lot of effort, you need to identify the right networks of people or powerful sponsors that you can align with in order to realize them. For some actions finding even one single like minded person with an identical goal can immediately multiply your results. It is also worth finding people who have already accomplished what you seek and asking for their advice and guidance.

While having major life goals and spending some time to reflect upon them has its benefits, obsessing over all of your daily actions may bring just the opposite effect where little actually gets done out of too much thinking and hesitation. Let's not forget that some of our greatest breakthroughs in life have been inspired on the whim of the moment, completely unplanned and unexpected.

One of the most precious dreams you can have in your life is that of remaining a child in your heart, where every new day is full of magic and amazement and sometimes, even if it's just for a moment, the perfect opportunity comes along, suddenly everything is possible, you make a wish upon a star and you are willing to give it a shot against all the odds.

THE FUTURE IS NOW

The answers to the future can be found in the moment, yet so many people seek them in the past

In medieval times, not quite so long-ago things used to be much simpler. If our grandfather was a blacksmith, chances were we and our grandchildren could live a full life by carrying over the family tradition and profession. Nowadays however, no profession seems to be stable enough to last us a lifetime or lately even a mere decade. The question then becomes, what can we do to set ourselves a direction for our future, so we don't end up in a dead end street?

To try and predict everything about the future is a futile effort, we can however take a step back and observe if our current beliefs and actions are pointing us in the right direction.

My main goal within these pages is to offer thoughts on how to do this most effectively so we can create a fulfilling future. I will try to set the main premise for a future built upon the balance of logic vs emotion and left-brain vs right brain. It is only by achieving this balance that we can hope to discover the spiritual or greater meaning of our lives. In each subsequent chapter I will focus in more depth on key areas.

In the year 2005 I was having the most important interview of my life and I was well aware of it. It was an interview for a 1st level position in the new IBM delivery center in Brno. It was not so much the position itself as much as just becoming part of this huge corporation that was enticing me greatly. My thinking at the time was that with the advance of IT the world would be in dire need of ... network specialists ... and by network specialists I mean the IP, routers, AT&T, Firewalls and Cisco guys. Thinking back about this prediction and my thinking at the time, I am realizing that I did get the first part right. The future was going to be about increasing connectivity and collaboration and network specialists are indeed in dire need but I was simply not thinking how this would change the social interaction of people and their emotions as well. The main mistake I was making was that I was simply basing my prediction on how things had changed in the past, not the potential of the situation at hand. There are all kind of network specialists these days that didn't exist just 10 years ago. Think about all the social media experts and Internet public relations specialists.

Why would such a negligent prediction matter for us today in our everyday lives and jobs? For one, because it is the perfect example of a prediction made only through IT knowledge and logic, without taking into account the emotional and social potential of the coming changes. By learning to take into account and apply both the logical and emotional views to your predictions in your own life you increase your chances of getting the right direction leading to a more fulfilling job and life.

Since the invention of the computer, all the progress until recently has always been focused and driven by logic, functionality and performance. As much as I don't like Apple products for their lack of said logic, functionality and performance, they have been the most successful IT company in the last decade because they were the first ones to focus to the emotional and visual sides of everything they made. It is my strong belief that the future of the next 7 years will be increasingly focused on realizing and manifesting the right brain needs of people and with this many professions will need to change to meet these demands.

Another trend that I believe we will see is the increased blurring of professional and personal life. More and more people are starting to take large parts of their jobs with as much love and passion as they have for their hobbies and that is a great thing. Current statistics indicate that as much as 80% of people do not enjoy their jobs and suffer lower productivity because of it. There is a choice here and it is not a very difficult one as well.

Let's have a look on how you can apply this mindset to your own job and personal life at this moment by asking yourself the following few key questions.

What are the logical and data driven concepts of my professional position? Have they changed in the last few years in any direction?

What can I do to introduce more creative, emotional and right brain concepts into my existing position? How is this going to improve the satisfaction of my peers and clients?

Is there a creative hobby in my personal life that can help me introduce more right brain concepts into my professional life?

How should I modify my personal development plan if I need more development in my right brain abilities?

The key to understand here is that right brain concepts are fun, enjoyable and creative by definition. Maybe even more importantly, do not make the same mistake I made a long time ago by trying to fit your 10-year goals within the current existing positions and limits of society. What you can do is try to set a direction that encourages growth on both the left brain and right brain concepts. Do not only focus on certifications, IT knowledge and core skills. Try to introduce as much as right brain concepts as you possibly can. The key to understand here is that right brain concepts are fun, enjoyable and creative by definition. The more of them you manage to fit into your daily life, the happier you are and the more love you have for what you do.

REFLECTIONS FROM THE PAST

Those who can't change their past are doomed to repeat it

Have you ever looked back into your life and hoped that things could've somehow turned differently? That you could have taken a different turn at the crossroads of life or that you could have at least taken a different approach? What if you were given the chance to change all that? Would you take it?

We have often heard the expression that the future is not set in stone, that anything and everything can be changed. What if I were to tell you that the past is also not set in stone and that anything and everything about it can be changed too without even owning a De-Lorean? Would you believe me?

When I was a kid and later a teenager in high school, I was completely fascinated by three things in life: computers, space and time travel. Of these three, the possibility of time travel probably fascinated me the most and I would spend countless hours dreaming and thinking of the concepts of time, studying the theory of relativity and watching

Back to the Future more times than I can possibly remember. Thinking back, what appeared to me most fascinating was not only the illusion of time but also its butterfly effect and how such seemingly insignificant actions in the present could have huge repercussions in the future.

My thinking was, which remains with me to this day, if I were to somehow understand how these small actions in the past contributed to the whole, then I would be able to control my small actions, and the actions of others, in the present and yield huge results given enough time. It dawned to me that each of us yields incredible power to change the future. Where others searched for that big jackpot and buried treasure that would change their life over night, I searched for that small dime which given enough time would compound itself to a million. As the years went by, I started discovering that the past is not set in stone and that we can actually go back and change certain aspects of it with immediate effects in our present.

Those certain aspects are the emotions, feelings and lessons we have in our minds and hearts deeply ingrained and chained with certain events in our past. We may not be able to change the physical events themselves but reflecting and changing on how we feel and how we understand something that happened in our past can have lasting and powerful immediate effects on our present understanding and emotional well-being. Let's have a look at few simple steps that we can apply to any single event in our life, process the emotion and take its lesson.

Try to visualize and focus on one, currently perceived negative, powerful event that you had in your past. Go as far as you would like, including your childhood, as when we are children, we tend to have extremely powerful emotions that continue to live with us even for somewhat trivial events. Focus on something that really left you feeling disappointed, lost, hopeless, confused and generally just made you feel like a total failure. Before you go ahead naturally wishing this event away as if it never happened and trying to forget about it, please bear with me and try to process it through the following few steps. Realize that nothing is ever truly forgotten and it continues to live on in our subconscious mind having lasting effects in our present and future.

Acceptance - Imagine all the positive aspects and success that you have right now in your life. Find those few key aspects that make you wake up each morning and make you feel that your life is worth living for.

Regret - You may be wishing this event never happened. Imagine what would happen to your life if that powerful negative event didn't happen. Would you be in the same place you are right now? Would you be the same person you are right now? What would you lose if this event never happened? Without this event to teach you a powerful lesson, would you be much more vulnerable for a much worse version of it in your future?

Gratitude - Once you have accepted where you are and stopped wishing for things to have happened differently you actually start feeling gratitude for that event. In this instant you effectively change your past by changing all those negative emotions tied to this one single event, releasing you to go to the next step and without the bias of emotions finally take the lessons from it objectively.

Lessons – Without the negative emotional burden, think about all the positive lessons this event has brought to you. What did you learn from it and how did it make you a better person? How would you approach the situation if it was presented to you again in the future?

Dreams - With the emotional charge changed to positive and the lessons taken, now we are free to dream and visualize the future without any fear of failure as failure does not really exist. It is only an assigned emotion to certain events in our past and projected future due to our limited point of view.

If you keep applying this mind exercise to events in your past, either professional or personal, you start to realize that your past is now looking very much differently than it did in the past and the future may be looking brighter than ever. Every time you change the way you feel and understand your past, you have also effectively changed it and by doing so created a small butterfly that changes the future in more powerful ways than we can ever hope to understand.

The most important of all however is that you start to realize that no matter what you do in life and no matter what events come your way, there is always a light at the end of every tunnel and you always come out of it a better and more evolved person than when you entered it.

INSPIRATION VS. ILLUSION

We have heard it a thousand times: "It is about the journey, not about the destination". You shouldn't be bothered if you succeed or fail as long as you are happily journeying. Hmm? Really?

Looking back at our lives, each of us will find many cases where we have had great inspiration to do certain things only to find out later that they did not reach our original expectations. On the other hand, sometimes we have been inspired to do something that doesn't make any sense whatsoever in the moment, but it has lead us to results beyond our wildest imaginations. How can it be that inspired actions can lead to such different roads?

Is it really possible to put such a wild and unpredictable force under control and reap only the positive benefits of it? Wouldn't it be the greatest thing in the world if we could somehow recognize the truly inspired actions vs the ones based on plain illusion?

By nature, I have always had an impulsive character, blindly following my heart and taking action in the moment without giving it a second thought as long as I had felt inspired. Needless to say, I had learned very quickly that this road has had its downfalls as well and that the inspiration of the moment had been nothing else but an illusion. Even worse, I had realized that my inspiration had not even been my own but that of someone else's making. The alternative would be no better however, thinking, analyzing and putting rationale behind every action I would take? That is surely not the answer either. Last time I looked in the mirror I did not see a robot in there. It is the age-old question of heart vs mind, passion vs logic, the journey vs the destination.

These days it is so easy to get an inspiration or rather an illusion impulse wherever we go. Let's face it, management theory has figured it out hundreds of years ago and companies are not afraid to use every trick they have in their books. When a person is inspired, they will stop at nothing until they achieve the object of their inspiration. They will even gladly do it for free or for very little in return because the action itself is the biggest reward they can get. Isn't that the perfect deal? What can we do to protect ourselves from those that want to hijack our true inspiration and replace it with their own? How do we see the difference between true inspiration that comes from our own hearts vs the illusion that has been put there by the world around us?

The answer is very simple, and it is actually a question. Never be ashamed or afraid to ask yourself or the ones that are trying to inspire you:

"What's in it for me? What do I get out of this deal? What do I really get at the end of day about being inspired about something in particular?"

This is where you really have to start thinking logically if the results of this undertaking really are in your best interest and if that's really the best you can get. If the possible results are not yet clear, then perhaps the whole thing is not that solid after all. The very least you could ask yourself if by the end of the day, that whole inspired undertaking will at least make you a better person.

It sounds really simple yet I see people every day, that are ready to jump into something that kind of feels good or simply because it is being led by someone charismatic or because they don't want to hurt someone's feelings or they even try to convince me to do it with them but then when I ask them about what kind of real benefits am I going to get, there is little to no answer. Often, they are not even able to answer what are the benefits they are getting out of it themselves.

True inspiration always comes from the heart but is also always supported by the mind. If you are not living and being inspired by your own dreams, chances are you are living someone else's dream with an illusion to guide you. Inspiration should be the lighthouse that guides you on your journey, not the shackles that bind you.

COMMERCIAL EDUCATION VS MARTIAL ARTS

Welcome to the real world, Neo

For many years I have had this small hobby of developing and facilitating commercial workshops in the area of management. This means workshops targeted at business managers with the end goal of increasing their performance. I have mainly done this for IBM and few other institutions including the Masaryk university and Brno University of Technology. I have had over 3000 participants over the years with a total very satisfied rate of 93%, 7% 'only' satisfied and virtually zero neutrals or dissatisfied or very dissatisfied. I don't mean to brag at all for all the reasons you will read below, satisfaction rate just says that people had a good time, but I'd just like to say that I've been around the block when it comes to commercial education.

Back in 2015 I received a special offer for an Agile workshop lasting 8 hours for the special price of 600 EUR (travel not included). The sad thing is that many companies will just blindly send their people just because the organizing company has a 'good name' and has received very positive feedback from participants. Rarely anybody cares for the only feedback that matters. Did people actually learn something that could not be found online and did their real performance improve? Let me tell you, if I am ever going to pay 600 EUR for an 8-hour workshop it better be lectured by Superman and it better contain the secrets of the universe and beyond.

The real problem with commercial education today is that it is obsessed with participant satisfaction with little regard of actual skill gained. Many lectors simply don't bother too much, and they conduct a care bear workshop where everybody wins, nobody really learns anything new but hey, we are all FEELING GOOD by the end of it. Now don't get me wrong, feel good workshops are great for specific purposes but you can't have a workshop about senior management negotiation and be nice about it the whole time.

I try to be a rebel in this system and actually try to teach people even at the risk of them giving me a lower satisfaction. What many lectors don't realize though is that most people are starting to see through the whole care bear feel nice workshop facade and really do want to learn something new even at the expense of some temporary pain. At the end of the day, they rise above it a better person than they came in and provide an even higher SAT rating than the average. I can't count how many times I've gotten the feedback at the end: "Finally someone told us the truth!".

If you remember the kung-fu movies of the 70s/80s it was very apparent that in order to actually have a big breakthrough and really learn something, you need to experience a certain pain under the hands of your tutor. No pain, no gain they say in the world of martial arts. Apart from the obvious joke about old kung-fu movies, there is some truth to this.

Breaking down old systems and habits IS painful, and this includes management practices. I did martial arts for 3 years and let me tell you, nobody gave us any feedback form to say how satisfied we were with our tutor on our last class. No, we got a kick in the stomach... I do mean a literal KICK in the stomach strong enough to stop my breathing for a minute. I did NOT like my tutor for that, but I DID learn how to defend myself if that need ever came and I did learn how to take a literal kick in my gut.

How do I rebel against the current trend? Don't worry , I am not going to physically kick you :) but in my workshops you do learn the feeling of failure, dealing and raising above it and taking many lessons so that next time you see a similar situation in real life you are ready to take it by the horns. People are always shocked when I tell them that they have actually failed 50-70% of the exercise but then I tell them honestly: "Look, don't worry, the exercise is designed in such a way that most people fail a big portion. I know you are used to work-shops where they give you easy exercises, you win and feel good but this is the only way I am going to let you see your gaps and this is the only way I can customize this workshop to the exact needs of this group."

As a colleague of mine always says. Good lectors know the differ-ence of designing a workshop FOR the participants, not the other way around where many, too many lectors use the workshop only to show off to other people of how great and smart they are.

Next time you are going to sign-up for a 600 EUR workshop or maybe design your own workshop, you may want to ask yourself the following three questions:

1. Satisfaction rate is a great bragging point for the lector but do I really need to pay 600EUR just to feel good? What was the actual performance boost that participants had after taking this workshop?
2. Can I find the same information online or will this workshop grant me access to exclusive PRACTICAL information I can use in real life.
3. Is this workshop going to have me practice CHALLENGING ex-ercises where I discover my gaps and receive mentoring on the spot on how to overcome them?

These days it seems everybody is some sort of a coach, lecturer or facilitator with literally thousands of workshops available on any given subject enhanced by certification organizations.

Before you shell out your hard-earned money for a commercial education never forget one thing: They are not there to permanently teach you in a fast, simple and straightforward way. They are there to sell you as many hours of education as they possibly can. For them an hour of education is just a product and they want to sell as much of their product as they possibly can while maintaining your satisfaction rate through many 'feel good' and ego boost tricks they possibly can bordering on the line of psychological manipulation.

The slower you learn and the better you feel about yourself during their workshop, the greater the chance of a returning client for them.

EDUCATION

There is but one thing worse than being uneducated, following the teachings of a fool

In this chapter I would like to share with you some tips and tricks on how to recognize a good education course and a teacher whether online or classroom and how to build your own. When it comes to education, I can get some really strong, both positive and negative feelings. Let's just say it's a love & hate relationship. Before we get to that part, I would like to share some thoughts.

Do you know what education, dreaming, Dragons and new year's resolutions have in common for me? Dreaming is what I have mostly done during my high school and university years during boring lectures that I either never bothered to attend at all or, in case of mandatory attendance, managed to sleep through with my eyes open, daydreaming of relaxing on a beach somewhere, solving some extremely important problem in my mind.. like how to kill that end-boss dragon in the online game I played all night before said morning lecture. In those days, there were no laptops so unfortunately, I couldn't do it right away on the spot from the last row.

You see, that Dragon guards a secret magic robe that will allow me a higher amount of armor and resistance to magic, allowing me to kill other players at a much more efficient rate and become one of the most feared, evil and infamous mages throughout the lands of Eternia. People will tremble at the mere sight of my name in the distance. Having to choose between *that* or paying attention to an anti-social Math professor, right hand writing - left hand erasing, with self-worth issues on how to perform a Laplace Transformation. You get the drift. And no, I don't really care about the fact that without Laplace Transformation I wouldn't have my online game in the first place. I had decided I was going to be a manager and someone else would be figuring this one out.

As it has been 10 years since I have been out of university and my days and nights no longer involve chasing Dragons guarding magic items naturally my life has shifted towards more productive endeavors, like you know, chasing managers guarding magic resources that I need in order to become one of the most feared, evil and infamous manager in the lands of ... nevermind.

It is no secret that I am really not a big fan of formal education. This can be viewed as a paradox, perhaps even a hypocrisy as I have gained all the formal papers, I can including senior professional certifications. Most of you have already heard about the Magic of Project Management. It is a course I have designed and delivered over 20 times in the last 3 years. During this time by getting feedback from the participants and other lecturers I have discovered many tips & tricks of what makes an effective education vs. one that puts the participants in a comatose sleep. I have also been developing and teaching various other workshops and presentations and studying different teaching methods. What I have discovered during this time is that the main problem with formal education is that its quality can vary wildly and the changes towards better are painfully slow. There are some faculties and teachers with modern teaching methods that really get you forward while on the other hand there are institutions bogged down by dogma and methods literally centuries old with rigid professors too stubborn to change. The worst part is that in some cases a degree from the later kind could have a higher prestige than the former one.

Like it or not, educating yourself continuously has become a necessity for survival in this fast-paced world. I mentioned in the beginning that I would like to share some tips & tricks on how to recognize a good education course. Let's have a look.

Content - Ideally the content should be built upon sources that you can self-study or read online. It's a colossal waste of time when the lecturer just reads information you could read on your own.

Relevance - Is the content focused on the audience group you belong into? Does it help you solve daily problems, or it is more like a high arcana that you need personal consultations to translate it to normal daily language.

Experience - Is the content drawn on real life experience or just on a bunch of books somebody read or the theoretical musings of a lecturer who got their degree 30 years ago and never had any hands-on experience?

Visual & Audio - Is the formatting done in an effective way that feels nice to the eyes and lets you focus on the key message instead of having to take a break every 20 minutes due to poor formatting and design from the 50s created by a rusty typewriter?

Rhetoric Style of the Lecturer - Do they make the education fun, interactive and engaging? Ask around before you decide to waste a day of your life. I wish I had the last time I signed up for a 3 day education and had to leave in the first 4 hours due to the danger of seizure caused by extreme boredom and a lecturer that projected the charisma of a sleeping zombie trying to make dull and self-aggrandizing jokes.

Gamification - This stands for a relatively new concept of introducing game mechanics into the business and education world. Does the workshop involve playing games and beating the crank out of the other participants? I still haven't met a participant that didn't enjoy playing the games. Even those most resistant to learning can't help it but learn a thing or few. I guess it's difficult not to when you are the one getting beaten the crank out of.

The last step that I would highly recommend is trying to build your own education material. As the saying goes: *"If you want to perfect something, teach it"*. One simple rule above all that I highly recommend, and I personally like to keep in all my mentoring and teaching activities is to make them fun. Let's face it, there are thousands of distractions that always compete for people's attention. The only way to make sure people are listening is to make it fun and entertaining first. Don't forget to have fun yourself as well. It is one thing to be a boring lecturer but what usually puts the final nail in the coffin of a horrible education workshop is when the lecturer is bored doing it as well. Avoid attending such lectures at all cost.

INTENT – DO AS YOU WILL

If you don't know what you want, someone else will choose it for you

Few years ago, I had decided that the time had come to buy a car. First time around back in Macedonia I had bought a new Chevrolet Spark which I had sold couple of years later. While the Spark was a great car, this time around I figured that buying a used but bigger car would be the preferred option. There was just one small problem: I could hardly tell the difference between a diesel or petrol engine and could at best recognize the difference between a Skoda and Porsche. As far as I was concerned, cars were these canned things on four wheels roaming around the city and I never paid much attention to the differences between them. Here I was however, deciding to buy a new car. Let me share the journey I took between then and the moment when I finally parked a beautiful Hyundai i30 in front of my place.

As I normally do when trying to buy something or get myself into a new field, I undertook two steps. First, I tried to read as much as I can on the internet and then simply ask people around on their opinion. The first thing they asked me back is about what are my expectations from a car. Hmm... what you mean expectations? I need it to get me from point A to point B with minimum breakdowns and visits to the mechanics. Based on such ambiguous expectations the advice ranged from an old 2003 Skoda Superb all the way to a new Toyota Yaris. Not much help. Here is where I decided to use my own experience as a project manager to manage this whole labyrinth of decisions.

Make the requirements as specific as possible. Once I sat down and put everything on paper the choice came down to basically two brands. Volkswagen and Skoda

I started reading as much as I can on these two brands. Few things became very apparent. When it comes to cars, people are VERY emotionally tied to a certain brand based on what they have owned with complete disregard to statistics. "I don't care that these cars break down more often", they would say, "MINE didn't have a single problem". Now while I am happy for them, this didn't help me much with my choice. Still the choice was leaning towards Skoda Octavia 2 , year 2009+ as the best choice of a used car.

The decision was made, I reserved few cars from the biggest auto dealer, got an agreement with the brother of a friend who is a mechanic to check it out and went to see it. Imagine my surprise when the auto dealer point blank told me that the first two choices are no longer available, blown engine but the third one was available. After getting a test drive and making sure there are no obvious signs of tachometer manipulation, I arranged for my mechanic to see it. Everything checked out except for the final check at the bottom. There was a leakage of oil under the transmission and his experienced eye caught the signs that someone had already tried to fix it and failed! I was practically ready to buy this car and you are telling me it could have easily cost me 20% more on repairs? Obviously, a step back was needed here! I was more than helpful that I have used an important principle I have learned over the years as a manager.

Forget about all the advice given to you by friends, family, significant others. Focus on the advice of professionals that deal with your subject every day

I vaguely remembered that my friend is working in a Hyundai dealership. Suddenly a flash bulb went in my head. Why in the world am I buying a Skoda when I have here a guy who works in a Hyundai authorized dealership? Hyundai had come up earlier in my choosing process, but few stereotypes had taken it down before even being considered. Again, I remembered another principle that I should use:

Make a new objective analysis and don't rely on historical information. Things change!

His simple advice was that cars are not what they used to be, all the brands with few exceptions are more or less the same and that I shouldn't limit myself to Volkswagen and Skoda.

I was very pleasantly surprised to discover that Hyundai had made an incredible jump in quality and were basically in the Top 4 only behind brands like Porche and Jaguar! The cars were designed by an ex-BMW designer and produced right here in the Czech Republic. Oh, and btw, a 5-year warranty without any limit to kilometers driven.

But I didn't have a budget for a new car, and I had decided buying a new car is just not efficient. You wait for 1-2 months until it is delivered, and you lose 20% value practically as soon as you leave the dealership. How about a car from a used car dealership that is still under warranty? This is where I hit the jackpot as I saw that the used cars with only 30 000km aboard and 2 remaining years of warranty are as much as 40% off from the value of a new car. Amazing! I remembered another important principle from management.

Consider the context of the situation and always calculate the bottom line

Buying a used Skoda from 2010-2011 would have cost me about 20% less but factor into this the fact that for 2 years something would probably break down, worse mileage per gallon of fuel, no contacts in a specialized car service shop and maybe even more importantly while the Skoda made sense on paper... my intuition was screaming to me that Skoda is simply not my style! I don't even want to think about the fact that the chance of a serious problem is greater when buying from the used car dealerships as many people when they discover a hidden fatal problem, instead of spending a lot of money on fixing it, they rather just sell the car without telling anyone and buy a new one.

The next step was tricky. I had to go inside the lion's den. The biggest and most infamous used car dealership in the Czech Republic. Everybody I asked told me to watch out that these guys are sharks ready to eat and manipulate you at the slightest sign of weakness. Armed with theory and my friend next besides me as the specialist... it turns out I had very little to fear. Pretty soon they realized I had done my homework and based on that alone they spoke to me like equals and told me pretty much any information I asked about the car, simply because I told them I am brining a mechanic to double check. From here on, it went really fast. I chose a car, my friend checked it out and I decided to take it. It was time to go in and tell them I want it while trying to bring the price down. Again, it was time for some management techniques.

Use leverage when negotiating and play hard to get

The car was such a nice specimen and hard to find that I had put a reservation fee (totally refundable) the day before having it checked out by my friend. So my position was pretty weak as they smelled blood and knew I am interested in the car. It was basically impossible to find any technical flaws, plus the car having 2 more years of warranty. I put on my poker face and acted really disappointed that the back seat was scratched a bit and the paint was also scratched a bit on one of the sides next to the rear bumper. With my friend we had logged in to the Hyundai service center and found out the exact amount this would cost. It was ridiculously high but it gave me great arguments to fight back. At first of course they tried to play hard ball and say they can't put a single cent off the price. Then we went for plan B and my friend advised me to wait until tomorrow so he can check some other options. Combined with the flaws we found this new threat of me not making the sale today (which I had found out is the prime goal of every salesman, is to get you to buy today) their resistance cracked and they went to see the 'manager' to approve the discount. A normal trick being used. After the small theater we signed the deal. The battle was not over yet, it was time to check the fine print and 'added services'

Always investigate all of your options before committing to anything

They wanted to sell me two things during the contract drafting. The first was a bag with the mandatory equipment that any car should have (things like first aid kit etc). I flat out said no because I had no idea what the price of the kit is outside of the dealership. Rightly so, I got the bag for half the price elsewhere.

The second thing was the insurance on the car. I flat out said no as I thought it is another rip off, but none the less I told them to print me the offer. Using this offer as a leverage I was able to get the same price at another insurance dealer who added up assistance services completely for free. Turns out, they had some special arrangements with the insurance groups and the original offer was a great one. My agent had to try really hard to match the offer, but it only confirmed to me that in negotiations, it is all about the leverage and having options!

Just for kicks I told him to look up my car on the internal systems of insurance groups and see if the price I paid for the car was a good one (basically the price they would pay me if my car got stolen). I found myself leaving the office with a big grin as he confirmed that I had made a real good purchase.

And finally the 7th principle

Management techniques can be used to greatly enhance your personal life... and get you some sweet deals :)

At the time of publishing of this book I am still happily driving my car with no issues experienced whatsoever.

TRUE EXPRESSION

In the hall of mirrors, you can never hide even from yourself

In many ways, it is a paradox. We live in the information age where we have all the knowledge of our civilization at our finger tips yet we are surrounded by lies, manipulative marketing, public relations, official statements, contradictory opinions and all kinds of 'confidential' information that someone else decided for us that we don't have the need to know. How is it possible that with all that information at our disposal, truth and integrity have become a luxury?

While there may be many answers to that question, the only one worth asking is: How do we find the rays of sunlight, integrity and truth in this world of broken mirrors?

In the year 2008 I got nominated to intensive two-day management assessment training. The whole purpose of the assessment being: To be observed by 6 senior managers about our ability to communicate, build relationships, manage and lead other people.

Wanting to make the best of it, I spent weeks in preparation, asking other people about the structure and format of the assessment and reading all kinds of articles on those topics. Long story short, I failed.

The main failure was not the negative assessment I got at the end but it was the fact that I did not properly express what was really inside of me in those two short days as I was always watching my behavior and being afraid of how I would be perceived by the observers. The reasons for the negative assessment were too many to count but one sentence summed it all up as one of the senior managers, a nice and compassionate lady, on the final feedback session asked me a very simple question that stroke me right in the heart and to which I was completely clueless for an answer that all those articles did not prepare me for:

"Evel, what makes you happy? I had not seen you smile during the last two days."

An angry part of my young self in that moment wanted to scream: "What the hell does that have to do anything with this assessment?" … but a much bigger, and sadder part of me, knew better.

Fast-forward to the year 2014, month of May and here I am going to the same assessment for a second try. I still may not have everything I would wish or need in my life or the perfect skills for a manager but one thing is for sure, I had 6 years to think about what makes me happy and 6 years to remember to always smile no matter how tough or serious the situation. This time there would be no preparation, no reading of countless of articles, only two casual conversations over coffee with couple of colleagues that have been there in the previous months so I could get a feel of what to expect. Long story short, I succeeded.

The main success was not the positive assessment I got at the end but even before I got it I had decided the whole experience had been a success for the very simple reason that this time I fully expressed how I really thought and how I really felt without stressing over the observers' opinions. Whatever came next would only be a mirror of that and would help me further grow. Most important of all, after 6 years of contemplating, I had finally figured it out. Being who I really am, expressing how I really think and feel and being with people who allow me to do that without having to hide or pretend. This is what makes me happy above all, simply having the freedom to be who I really am.

Having the courage to do that at least with ourselves and those closest to us is the first step but there always seems to be a twist to the story. How do we keep true to ourselves and at the same time thrive in this world of broken mirrors and sandcastles without being taken advantage of?

Value - Before you even think, say or do anything, ask yourself the question as to what kind of value will it bring you? Is it something constructive that will propel your relationships to new depths or is it something based on negative emotions or perhaps completely useless?

Emotions - How emotional are you about it? There may be zero value at fighting with someone but if we avoid the fight we are still left with a lot of emotions that need venting. Find creative ways to vent negative emotions before they lead us to expressing things we may later regret.

Express - If you have decided there is real value in it then have the courage to fully express it. This includes fighting. Some battles are worth the fight. Go for it!

Reward - Welcome and reward people for telling you how they truly think and feel about you.

Mirrors - With every expression you make, there will be countless mirrors to reflect it back to you. These will be the words, reactions, faces, thoughts and feelings of others around you. Action - Reaction. Have the courage to look at your reflection in the mirror, learn from it and change if you don't like it.

Secrets - Use secrets wisely. The more you try to hide your real self, the more distorted will your image in the mirrors become, attracting all sorts of people that don't suit your real nature.

Trust - Be extremely careful at who you trust but be trustworthy yourself. It takes only one wrong step to crack a perfect mirror that can never be put perfectly together again.

Smile :)

In the quest for truth, above all, realize that the chapter above and this whole book is just my own truth being expressed as an image across the hall of mirrors. In this world of broken mirrors, infinite reflections and sandcastles that can disappear overnight the only truth that really counts for each and every one of us is the one in the middle, inside our hearts. Have you asked yourself what makes you happy and what makes you smile?

CROSSROADS

It's not who you are underneath, it's what you do that defines you

Christmas is definitely a unique period of the year for many reasons. My favorite ones are that the pace of the entire world slows down, and I am able to see much more clearly about what has happened in the last year and make some major decisions of where should I be heading in the next one. I am not talking about some shallow new year's resolutions but decisions that affect the very core of my life and which I have every year always seen though until the very end. This blog post may be a bit darker and murkier than the previous ones but let's make one thing clear, tough decisions always come at a price.

Efficient decision making is probably one of the most underestimated areas when it comes to management, leadership and life in general. Most people will agree that whether it comes to deciding what present to buy or deciding who lives and dies in a time of war, it is important to make the right one. The reality however is disappointing as in many cases people miss big opportunities because of inefficient decision making yet other times it is amusing as their own hesitance and indecision opens the doors for myself and others who are bolder to take the shot.

One of the most difficult and at the same time one of the easiest decisions I have ever had to make when it comes to the work environment was probably in the year 2008. I was working in a Macedonian company and was asked point blank by my boss to fire one person from a team of three people because of budget restrictions. The special 'Balkan' contracts allowed an immediate firing day to day of the person without any special reason. I had spent several months with these people, going to lunches and some team buildings so it was very difficult to approach things rationally and objectively. However, once I stripped the decision away from all the personal emotions surrounding it and focused on the business results and background, the picture became very clear and I was able to decide within 15 minutes. The fired person was in tears half an hour later but as they say, it comes with the territory. It was not an easy discussion that followed but until this day I believe I made the right call.

Let's see how to approach the decision-making process and make sure that we are getting the most out of the cards we are dealt with.

Vision - You must have a vision of where you want to be, a certain goal or an ideal upon which you will weigh every decision. Is the decision bringing you closer to your goal or getting you further away?

Alternatives - What are the options of this decision and what are the positive and negative impacts that they bring.

Lines - How far are you really prepared to go? What are the lines you will never cross? Keep an open mind though as the lines are never set in stone and experience, circumstances or other people can easily shift them.

Preparation - Are you really prepared for the negative consequences of your decision? Most tough decisions, no matter how wisely made always have a negative component that you will be left to deal with.

Boldness - Once you have made up your mind, there is no turning back. Decisions must be made with boldness and seen all the way through until the end unless of course mid-way you realize you have clearly made a bad decision.

Bad Decisions - Sooner or later you will make a decision that will be a bad one, not necessarily because of a mistake on your side, hurting yourself and others around you. A wise leader is able to pick the pieces from the floor, acknowledge the change of circumstances or admit their own mistakes (even if only indirectly) and make yet another bold decision with the intention of setting things right.

Ghosts - Major decisions are like ghosts – Good ones will stay with you until the end of your life to inspire self-confidence with the bad ones to haunt you with fear and self-doubt. As a leader you must make peace with the ghosts of past, learn from them and set sail forward into the future.

Realize that at the end of the day it doesn't really matter what is underneath your heart and mind and what your real intentions were. It is your actions that will define you and the people you lead. Every strong defining action is by necessity preceded by a bold decision so be sure to make it a wise one of your own making.

THE POWER OF WHY

It is purpose that connects us, purpose that created us, purpose that defines us

A while back, a friend called me: "Hey, let me call you and tell you about my project". My reply was: "I don't want to hear about your project, I am watching a movie (I was not even watching a movie at the time)". The main problem he forgot to think about was one simple question, why would I care about his project in the middle of a Sunday afternoon?

Generally, I like to think that I meet three types of people throughout my life with regards to the positive value they can bring. Let's face it, since the invention of the internet and since it has given access to direct contact with over a billion of different people at any single point, the value of being in contact with anyone for the sake of being in contact has severely degraded.

The first type is people who are right on the mark, they tell me what they are all about in under 5 minutes and just as easily tell me directly or at least give me an indication of how I will benefit by spending time with them, the benefit being either material, emotional, knowledge based or whatever other positive value they are able to offer.

Then there is the second type of people, who even though are quite interesting, they are simply neutral, without much touching points we can share. No harm done as long as we both realize this and part ways.

The third type however is the worst. Those are people who come to me with points that have absolutely no positive value to bring to me, yet they try and push them forward, sometimes without even telling how it benefits anyone in the world, let alone themselves. I can't count the number of times I've been on a meeting or in the pub with such a person with a single though on my mind while trying to send all kind of non-verbal signals that I am bored as hell "Please oh please just shut up."

All this may seem rather harsh and cold, but as I said, contact with people is becoming even more frequent with all the latest increases of communication channels so we must make sure to make best of the limited time we have to initiate real quality contact. The first rule is actually very simple. Either give the other person in under 5 minutes what you are all about and what is your current interest with them or guide them and ask them to do the same to you. Look for non-verbal signals, if someone has not said a word for the last 10 minutes and are gazing with their eyes on all kind of places except your face, chances are they are trying to tell you to stop or change subject.

In Operations and sometimes in Project Management when things go FUBAR, management will ask you to initiate a root cause analysis. This means to investigate what caused the whole chain reaction that led to the current problem. The same applies to people, if someone tells you they need anything from you, don't settle to provide them the thing they need (unless you just want to get rid of them quickly and effortlessly). If you really want to help them and build quality rapport with them, try and dig deeper and find what is the root cause they want this thing in the first place. This is the single best advice I can give you for building high quality contacts of people who will be always happy to talk to you gain and cooperate.

At the end of the day, we are all complex people with complex lives (at least most of us) and splitting our personality into a person vs business individual is not easily achievable or very healthy. Don't be afraid to always mix business with pleasure and get the most fun out of every contact you make. If you are meeting a colleague don't get stuck and think only in terms of how to make the next report better. Try to get to know the person behind the role and then speak to the person, not the role they are covering. If your meeting is ending 10 minutes earlier, don't rush for the door but spend the next 10 minutes expanding the scope of the conversation to non-business topics, you may be amazed at how much more added value it will bring to your business connections. In all my time in professional life and outside, the best colleagues I've had were always the ones with whom I could speak on so many other topics other than business. Only then it was possible to achieve the most out of our common business topics and work together more efficiently. Just the same people will go above and beyond to help you out if they are speaking to the person in you, not only the role you are covering.

THE SANDS OF TIME

There is but one certainty in life, its inevitable end

Time is the only thing in life that can't be bought, traded, given or taken away. You can rule the whole world, but it won't make any difference to the time available to you on a given day, month or a year. With time being the most precious commodity in your life, have you asked yourself if your time is well spent and not wasted? Have you found yourself feeling you don't have enough time for everything you would like to do? Have you had people, friends or your own team in your projects, turn you down with your requests for the reason of 'not enough time for you'?

Why is it that certain people seem to always be relaxed and always have a lot of time at their disposal, even though they are quite successful in life by all means, yet others always seem to be under stress and in a rush, continuously in a lack of time?

Before I go any further, some of you may be starting to think: "Oh no, not another time management book, I don't have time for this stuff". I get it, I really do. I will be first to raise my hand in protest when given any time management strategies as I know very few people that have actually managed to use them effectively. We need to expand on the logical aspects of any system we want to use and start introducing emotional or right brain concepts in order for it to better integrate with the totality of our life. Let's call it Emotional Time Management where all time spent is like flying across rainbows, rivers of milk and honey and... well no, not really, let's get down to earth for a moment, shall we? :)

The real beauty of ETM is that by introducing emotions into the process, we make it more enjoyable, something to look forward to rather than yet another 'Have to do' item or a chore on our busy schedule. I am again the first one to protest over building detailed lists of our lives and following them. We are not robots to live our lives enslaved to a strict schedule full of numbers and priorities. Where is the beauty of spontaneity or the 'whim of the moment inspiration' in such a life? The whole purpose of doing such a list is just to get you into the right mindset. After the right mindset has kicked in, you won't need any lists anymore except maybe a very basic one of some major tasks.

Before jumping ahead, we need to first do some clean up in our hectic life schedule. You can do it yourself right now by following me on this short exercise. After a while of trying out this exercise, the filtering and prioritization should be happening automatically as you start to internalize the process. Kind of like learning to play the guitar or typing with all 10 fingers or filtering out what people are saying on a boring meeting and minding your own business (good time saving strategy right there!). Taking this to the next level, you can additionally use these insights not only to your schedule but also to get things done by people who continuously turn you down with the reason that they don't have time for you.

Make a list of all your actions on a given busy day where you felt you didn't have much time. Make sure to include small things like going for a coffee break, travelling to work etc.

Let's go through the list and apply several strategies to make it shorter on each of the actions. I call it the ACT WID system. I will not discuss effectiveness here because it is common sense that each action should be made as effective as possible without taking away any pleasurable concepts from it.

Avoid - Go through the list and see what was the real need behind the action, can this need be substituted by another less time-consuming action? What are you really going to lose from your life, logically or emotionally if you cut off this action completely?

Combine - Can any two actions be combined together? For example, reading the news or checking your Facebook on your cell phone while on the tram, instead of just staring at the road.

Transfer - Can you get someone else to do it for FREE or in exchange for your help with something they are not good at. At work this can be solved through smart delegation, in personal life by exchanging favors with friends who are much better at the task we have.

Wait - A well-kept secret of effective people is waiting until the last moment in the hope that someone else will do it, that it will no longer be necessary, or the requester will forget about asking you to do it. Use at your own risk and indiscretion! :)

Invest - Time is the most precious thing in your life. Think about finding a paid service for your problem. Even if it's something as trivial as buying gyros today or ordering a pizza rather than spending an hour cooking. Try to look at it as an investment in your quality of life, not a purchase.

Do It! - When all else has failed, some things you simply have to do yourself. By now the list should be a bit shorter and containing only actions that you have to do yourself or simply want to do yourself because let's face it, having your friend go for a coffee break instead of yourself is not really the wisest time saving strategy of all time :). Let's add more detail to the 'Do It!' list, nothing too complicated I promise :). You can use numbering from 1 to 10 to indicate this value.

Value - Some time management will tell you to introduce also Urgency vs Importance but seriously, nobody has time to do all that stuff on their lists. We usually know if a task is really valuable to be done today or not really.

Pleasure- How much are you going to enjoy this task? Is this something that is not really valuable in objective terms but brings you immense emotional satisfaction? Perhaps it is ideally both valuable and pleasurable?

Now it is all up to you and your personal preferences. Feel free to combine tasks and arrange them based on the mood at a given day. It's almost like baking a cake, you can have thousands of flavors. You can have days where you focus on value and other more relaxed days where you focus on pleasure. Personally, I prefer Wednesdays focused on value and Fridays focused on pleasure and the other days being a mix based on my current mood.

The key understanding you need to have is that it is never really about the lack of time. Time is the same for all of us, always has been, always will be. It is always about the lack of prioritization, organization and emotional insight in the ways that we live our lives.

TRUST – THE INNER CIRCLE

Real trust never asks for proof, it is simply there, unspoken

Once upon a time, I submitted the paperwork for my business trip to Bratislava. To those that have done the process at least once, you will know what I am talking about. By the 4th hour of filling paperwork so I can get approved/reimbursed to buy a train ticket I usually find myself asking the question of how much simpler would it be if my company simply … trusted me more? How much simpler would be if the only form I had to fill was one with a single question "How much did your train ticket cost? .. Thank you, here is your money"

It is always amazing to me how much we all speak about trust yet how much of the world around us is built of systems upon systems which sole purpose is to enforce that we stay true to our word.

Why is it so difficult for people to commit and stay true that we have the constant need of policing that? I leave the answer to that to the philosophers, but let's not give up on trust so easily and see how it can actually be a powerful ally. Let me try to make the case for trust and all the powerful benefits it can bring into our lives.

When I was a kid, it took me several years to find out that some people actually … lie… big time… even to those closest to them which is something that I just can't understand even to this day. The mindset of "trust everyone" quickly turned into "trust no one". By the time I got to University in the Czech Republic I started to realize that in the new foreign and hostile environment I would not get very far without learning how to trust again. Learning to really trust has been by far the most difficult thing I've ever had to do and at the same time the most rewarding as well. By the 2nd year of the university studies, somehow naturally I formed very close friendships with two other students with whom we remain very close friends even to this day and whom I trust completely. Forming that close inner circle with them not only allowed me to finish my studies with a lot less effort and bigger safety but it also gained me friends for life.

The key lesson I realized from these two friendships was that trust was not something one chooses to do or asks for, one day it is simply there as a result of years of shared experiences. The most important however was the realization of the importance of having an inner trustworthy circle. An inner circle is a small core group of people who are committed to the same goals as I am and who put our relationships above their personal objectives. In the case of my two friends from the student years, this would simply mean that each of us would never stop until all the three of us would succeed in a certain subject and that we would watch our backs. We were so strongly connected together that the others jokingly called us the holy trinity. Some people like reading books about three musketeers while we were living that life. Those kinds of relationships, during my student years, personal life and later in my professional life as well in itself to me will always be priceless and I consider them as one of my greatest accomplishments in my life.

I wish I could write a step by step guide on how to trust someone but in this case, it is not possible. Few months ago, I asked a close friend of mine on how he manages to completely trust his wife, the most difficult of trust-based relationships, especially in today's society with so many horror stories and shifted moral values. His answer was pretty simple: "Time and openly sharing everything that life puts ahead of us, the good and the bad, there are no shortcuts to trust"

It seems scary and maybe even counterintuitive at first. Putting ourselves in such a vulnerable and in some ways restricted position but let's have a look at all the benefits.

Commitment - when we say commitment the first reaction is usually negative of something that restricts us. But when the entire inner circle commits, the result is completely the opposite. There is a big sense of freedom, bigger than we can ever achieve alone in the knowing you can close your eyes and relax for a moment as the rest of the circle is watching your back. Knowing there is always someone to pull you back up when you fall.

Goals - Committing blindly to a person is slavery but real nobility is found in jointly committing to a common goal with others who share that goal which makes the accomplishing of the goal so much easier.

Powerful Team - There is always someone to cover our weaknesses and fighting off any adversaries is a lot easier when you are not alone against the odds.

Confidence & Safety - Strength lies in numbers. You fear less life around you and on the other side your adversaries fear you more as they know you have powerful allies.

Sharing - Whatever surprises or success life throws your way, one thing remains for certain. You won't have to face anything alone.

As is the case in many other areas of life, we attract around us what we are on the inside. We can never hope to achieve a trustworthy inner circle in any area of our life until we become trustworthy ourselves. While it is not realistic to be always completely honest and trustworthy to everyone that we meet in our life it is definitely possible to be that way to the people that matter to us the most, both personally and professionally.

RELATIONSHIPS

Don't look for the perfect relationship, focus on becoming the perfect partner

This is probably one of the most hotly debated topic at both professional and personal level. I will not hold back on this one and this chapter will perhaps come across a bit harsh as I explore the dark side of relationships. I am doing this because looking around I see that most people already feel the truth about relationships, but they tend to only focus on the positive messages and avoid the wake-up calls that desperately try to reach them.

The key to understanding and mastering relationships is to stop debating them with friends over beer & coffee and listen to the pros. I used to be pretty poor at relationships, both personal and professional and I used to talk about them over beer & coffee with well-meaning but ultimately clueless friends whose own relationships were a mess. I used to take advice from a certain friend about my own relationships until the moment where I had the privilege of spending 3 days with him and his girlfriend. I am by no means judging their relationship, it obviously has worked for them for years even if fighting and quarrelling is their middle name. I guess some people like it rough. The problem is that I would never want something like that for myself. The next question I asked myself was: "Why am I taking advice from someone whose path I actually do not want to follow?" Lesson well learned. No more discussions about relationships with friends & family.

As I got a bit wiser I spent a long time studying all kinds of sources since the beginning of history from some of the biggest masters that ever lived on this ever elusive topic and it took me even longer to understand the final truth about it that comes as no surprise at all. As Phil Collins sang: "It's a game of give and take". My problem? If a personal or professional relationship mattered to me, I used to rather naively give rather than take.

You see, when we care about something or someone, either a client or a partner or a very dear friend, the temptation is to put their needs above our own or in some cases if we are so close and take the relationship for granted, we do the complete opposite until we lose it and realize its true value it had for us. Either way is a straight first-class ticket to hell.

The next advice you will hear about relationships is that it is all about trust. Maybe. That is just one type of a relationship and it is usually in personal life or with few lucky professional ones. Marrying someone you don't trust would be, let's face it, kinda dumb. Professional life, however, requires us to have successful relationships with people we don't like, we don't trust, that see us as nothing but mere pawns in their schemes and hell sometimes we even think they are mentally challenged to say the least. Ahh, now here is where the mastery of relationships is to be found.

Creating and maintaining deep life-long relationships has been my key life goal that I have been working hard on for many years. Also, after several years of being successfully and happily married here are some key rules that I have discovered and observed over the years that have stood the test of time. The more of these are present in a relationship the more beautiful and harmonious it is.

Value - The more value you can provide the more options you have in the relationships being offered to you. Again, this seems to be a universal truth both in personal and professional life. The oldest and most common advice you will find after a failed relationship is to move on and focus on building your own value to the next level. After a while a whole new world of options opens before you.

Expectations - Make your expectations clear with the other party. Detailed and straight to the point. If the expectations are not being met, introduce improvement plans. If they don't work out, look for other opportunities. No exceptions! I am not talking professional life only.

Self Interest - Expecting everything and giving nothing is really not fair or sustainable. After asking yourself what you are getting out of that relationship the next question should be of what you are offering in return. Appeal to the other party's self-interest. A relationship where both parties are not mutually getting something out of it is destined to quickly fail or completely drain the other person until there is nothing left to take, leading to failure anyway.

Balance - Who is the dominating side in the relationship in certain situations and can you handle it? Depending on the relationship, you must be able to be either submissive or dominating. At work your official role should correspond with the dynamic of the relationship. In personal life? It depends on the personal preference but usually one of the partners takes the lead. Of course, this is very situational, and the roles can switch several times per day. It is all about the flexibility and ability to play both roles as the situation requires it. In the couple from the beginning of the chapter the girl would never admit a mistake or submit. One word - Horrifying.

Trust - Building a relationship upon trust is obviously beautiful and the preferred type of relationships you want to have in life at all levels. However, some people play dirty. Personal life is easy, you simply get rid of them. No exceptions. Professional life? You may not get that luxury. Focus on written communication and commitments and establish clear un-ambiguous expectations on both sides supported by your formal roles. Getting some 'witnesses' to attend your meetings is also not a bad idea, just in case there are any misunderstandings later.

Communication - I really don't even feel like having to explain the importance of open communication in any kind of a relationship, even the ones where trust does not exist. Don't forget that listening is a big part of it.

Emotions - Let's face it. Some relationships we have should have fallen apart a long time ago but for some emotional or perhaps hormonal reason we are still trying to maintain them. Do a strong self-critical analysis of each of your relationships. Are they still providing you the value they used to provide or are you hanging in there only for some emotional reason which is no longer in your best interest? Realize that any dysfunctional relationship is a huge block towards having a balanced one with someone else.

Competition - Everything and everyone is replaceable. No matter how deep the relationship and how complex the ties, there is always a way out and there is always someone else behind the doors of life around us to replace us or our partners if we grow complacent, start taking our relationships for granted and stop working on them. You think you are different? Just look around at all the broken companies, ex-friends and ex-couples who also thought they were 'different'.

At the end of the day a contract is just a piece of paper, a promise of commitment are just words spoken into the wind conveniently forgotten when no longer useful and a ring is just a piece of metal, sometimes with a shiny stone. Provided and received value out of the relationship is the only ultimate secret to long and satisfying relationships on all levels of life. As much as the movies would like to have us believe, there are no fairy tales when it comes to relationships and there are no happily ever afters. Anyone who has accomplished a 'happily ever after' will be quick to point out that it takes a lot of continuous hard work and commitment to maintain it. They will however be also quick to point out, that a successful relationship is the most beautiful, satisfying and valuable thing in the world you can ever hope to accomplish. Every relationship has its dark side too. Learn from it, transform and accept it for what it is without judgment.

SUCCESSFUL FAILURES

Harmony is not made by a single dominant tone, but the combination of many, complimenting and balancing each other

How often have you found yourself frustrated that things are simply not going 'your way' and just not panning out based on your expectations? How often have you started blaming yourself or even worse, others, for this perceived 'failure'? Have you thought about how we are bombarded with all kinds of happy ending movies, inspirational success stories and endless self-development books and educational courses focused on success and self-esteem? All this intense pressure creating unrealistic expectations on us, others and our perception of what real life should be like how successful we should be and how capable we actually are. When is the last time you defined what the word 'success' actually means to you? Is it just more social status and wealth or this transcends into all areas of your life?

In our quest and pressure from today's society for ever greater and faster success in all areas of life we tend to forget that having balance in life, also means having balance between failure and success. The question then becomes, not how to succeed, get as much as you can in life and have everything 'your way' but how to achieve the deepest balance possible with the failures, compromises and sacrifices you will inevitably have to make along the way.

The ideal proportion of a balanced success with failure is a personal choice. Some people like to compromise a lot for the value of building relationships and likeability while others are more self-oriented and prefer having things 'their way'. The key here is not to push for the highest proportion of success possible at all times but to find the ideal proportion based on your own set of values and maintain it as close to that ideal as possible. This balance alone based on your own values is the main key to having a content and happy life in general.

By understanding and accepting failure as part of life, you become much more approachable by others, more understanding of their failures, their values and their own desired proportions of success and failure. You start seeing people for who they really are and start having realistic expectations as a result which is the basis of all meaningful relationships in life.

Back in 2007, as part of my self-development program, I scheduled myself a meeting with a senior manager in IBM that was very popular at the time. He had more than 40 years of experience within the company and was considered by many a great people person as well. I do not remember well what went on in that meeting but I do remember

I was very surprised when he told me: "You know Evel, every day I wake up, come to work and make important decisions. If by the end of the day I have made 80% of the best decisions possible, I can consider myself to have had a successful day. You just can't get everything right."

Balance should not be achieved by lowering your expectations and having as a result few and less severe failures. That can only put you on a downward spiral with ever decreasing expectations. Quite the contrary, the only way to get better at balancing your life is to increase your expectations, reach higher success levels and suffer more severe failures along the way that will bring valuable lessons helping you set aim for even higher goals. Let's see how we can do that in our daily lives with these simple steps:

Do not chase success for the sake of success or pure ego. Be honest with yourself and find the ideal proportion of the amount of success you want in a given field. Be aware that every time you succeed in a certain field, this means you have to sacrifice your energy and time from another one. It's a game of give and take.

Take the right amount of risk. Do not bet your house on anything in life. Make sure you can afford to suffer a certain failure and there is enough success to balance it out.

Never make the same mistake twice. Welcome failure in life but make sure that you never repeat the same exact mistake.

Have a strong vision of your direction. Never sacrifice long-term sustainability for any quick wins or quick fixes. Long-term success always takes time and effort that may not be apparent in the early stages and may even be perceived as failure at first.

Maintain your balance. Sooner or later, the balance will tip in either direction from your ideal position. Sometimes this is necessary for short periods of time but if this becomes a long-term trend, it may be time to take a step back and re-evaluate your approach.

Achieving this inner balance and harmony throughout your life has profound effects not only on how you feel about yourself but it also provides you with a far more realistic picture on your true capabilities and allows you to better judge when setting new goals and taking up on new challenges and opportunities. It provides the foundation for the most important belief in life, the belief in yourself. It acts like a compass that can guide you through those tough times when the whole world seems to be against you. In our quest for harmony in our life, we should always remember that harmony is not a single dominant tone, but the combination of many, complimenting and balancing each other.

SOLUTION MASTERY

Have you ever considered what would you do if just like Aladdin, you happened to find a magic lamp with a Jinni granting you 3 wishes? Have you ever thought what are your top 3 problems in life that you would finally like resolved but short of finding a magic lamp they just seem impossible to solve?

Maybe the problem is not really the problem but the problem maybe is your attitude about the problem? *(Credits go to Jack Sparrow for that one)*. The good news here is that if there is anything in life that we have control over, that is the power of our attitude.

In 1999 I spent a year in the beautiful Czech City of Podebrady, together with students from 100+ other nationalities where we were preparing in the Podebrady Castle for the entrance to a Czech University of our choice. In the dormitories where we were living, there was only a single TV room on the 3rd floor that was being closed and locked every day exactly at midnight no matter if there happened to be only 10 minutes left from a movie. While some receptionists were kind enough to let us stay longer, there were others that thoroughly enjoyed kicking us out while giving us an evil grin that I will never for-get. As you could imagine, there were many possible solutions to this 'problem' but as usual, the simplest and cheapest one proved to be most effective. After some brainstorming with my roommate, we fig-ured out a way to make a copy of the key to the room from a can of tuna by cutting it with scissors in the exact form of the key.

We perfected the process on the keys of our own room and then it was just a matter of borrowing the key from the reception for few minutes to open the door in the morning, draw its shape on the can and cut it later. This way we could just go back shortly after midnight, re-open the room, re-lock it from inside and keep watching movies all night. Few weeks into it, we decided to invite in our small secret circle also another friend who owned a Play Station 1 but did not have a TV. Not only did we solve our 'problem' but it also opened new possibili-ties for us, such as playing video games until the early morning hours.

While this small anecdote may seem silly in today's context, back then, in that specific situation it meant the world to us. There was no personal internet and laptops. Owning a PC was a major investment that hardly any of us could afford and cell phones were these gigantic bricks with ten letters on the screen. The point being made here is that when you look back, what we consider as trivial today, such as running water and heating, used to be a matter of life and death not so long ago and in certain parts of the world, it still is. Next time you face a problem that may seem epic in proportions, rest assured to the fact that it is only a matter of time before its solution is not only found but it also becomes trivial. It is all about finding the right keys to the locked doors we face in life.

Let's have a look at how you can not only find the right keys, but open those doors with ease as well.

Define - what the real problem is and make sure everybody understands. All too often we go on under the assumption that everybody understands what the real problem is until it is too late in the process and then we have to re-work everything.

Discover - the human need and emotion behind the problem. Most of us don't really need a blinking piece of plastic with many colors on its screen and more functions that you can ever hope to use. What most of us really need is a tool with which we can find and share information in the simplest manner. This is one of the major reasons why Nokia and Microsoft missed the boat and got slaughtered by Apple. Not enough focus on the user and underlying human needs behind the technology.

Seek - world-class professional guidance. Its natural and instinctual to ask for guidance and help from our close friends and family. While this may be emotionally helpful, in the vast majority of cases it is vastly inferior compared to getting world-class professionals on the table who have faced and solved similar problems many times already. With the internet, finding professional guidance and information has become very easy.

Customize - the solution. Even the best generic solution to a given problem can always be improved by customizing it to the exact situation and context you are facing. As they say, the devil is in the details. Do not be afraid to trust in yourself for the final minor modifications.

Take action - and improve the solution. Do not spend days of trying to find the perfect solution before taking any action. If the situation allows, put whatever solution you have on the table as soon as it is usable or perform trial tests in a safe environment. Feedback from trying out the solution in real life will give you more information than days of thinking and discussing it over. Nothing beats the good old trial & error attitude.

Perhaps the most important of all, is a shift of mindset. Look beyond the immediate reward of a solved problem. Each time you do find a solution the greatest reward is your increase of knowledge and expertise which is worth beyond anything that money can buy. There is nothing more rewarding in life than the knowledge that other people need your guidance and will wholeheartedly reward you for it, both emotionally and materially.

Once you start pushing the world-class boundaries of your chosen field of expertise you become essential not only to those closest to you but also to the entire world and then the ultimate challenge becomes about inspiring and empowering others to do the same ... but that my friends is another tale for another time.

COURAGE & BELIEF

There are no wrong paths to the one who believes in one self and has the courage to follow them

From the youngest age, most of us are taught to believe in ourselves, not listen to other people's opinions and just follow our dreams. Most children around us seem to believe in that. Why is it than that most of the adult humanity today seems to be in a permanent state of stress, fear of the future and lack of self-esteem and confidence? Do you believe in every step you take and face the challenges confidently or find yourself doubting in fear of what will happen next? What can we do to reclaim that childhood belief that we are worthy and capable of handling anything in life?

In one of my chapters I mentioned learning the basics of skiing and the lessons I learned doing so. In the weeks that followed, there were more powerful lessons that taught me more about increasing the belief in my growing abilities and tackling even the scariest of downhill runs at a faster speed than I ever believed I could handle safely in such a short period of time.

My last skiing trip I was fortunate enough to visit Flachau - Ski

Amade – one of the biggest ski centers in Europe. My friend has been skiing since he has been a small kid so the first hours on the slopes proved quite challenging for me in my ability to keep up with him.

After I had learned how to get to the bottom of a hill in a more or less controlled manner, I was still struggling on certain steep hills called black runs (There is a reason these white snow slopes are called black). On the way up with the lift, I would look at the hill and see how steep and long it is from the distance. I could almost hear my mind speaking in the background saying to me: "You don't have the experience yet! You need more time! You can't handle that scary steep hill! You don't have to risk anything!". The first two trips up, my friend could not convince me to join him on the black run as I would make up some excuse that the softer red run is more fun anyway. But I started thinking about how would I gain more experience and overcome my fears if I always gave up and went to ski with the kids on the softer slopes? It became crystal clear that if I ever wanted to take that last step, I would have to overcome my last fear and doing that tomorrow would be no better than today.

As I went for my first black slope, I will never forget the feeling while looking down from the top. It seemed almost impossible to me that I would be able to make it down without ending up sliding on my back instead of my skis. The solution was far simpler than I ever thought possible. Focus on the next turn taking it step by step without thinking about the whole slope. One turn after another, before I even had a chance to think about the whole thing, I realized I was half way through it and even enjoying it! In fact, in some ways it was even easier than the less steep runs as it was wider, less used and with natural snow!

As I made it down to the bottom, I realized how many times in my life I had been so scared of a big project, complex situation, scary meeting or a certain person – personal or professional. I had been so scared because I had been thinking about the whole thing as one huge overwhelming step and all the ways it could go terribly wrong, without focusing on the smaller steps first. In many cases in such situations the fear itself would make sure that I would fail spectacularly as I would try to tackle the whole thing in one go, not having the patience or confidence to take it step by step. Such failures would naturally make me doubt in my own abilities, increase my fear in similar situations and make it even harder to succeed the next time. Luckily, I have not made the same mistake so far on my journey down the skiing slopes. How can we get out of that vicious cycle of failures and doubt in our own abilities?

Limitations - Know your real ability, confidence and current situation. Always be brutally honest at what you can really handle. Forget about the movies where a nobody turns into a savior of the world in 2 hours flat. You are a real human being not a super-hero.

Step-by-Step - Once you have identified what is your real ability, set your aim for the next level. Make it challenging enough so that you can improve but not too challenging that it becomes dangerous and a risk to the entire undertaking.

Safe Environment - Experiment with levels far above your current ability but do it so in a safe testing environment. Even if you are not able to handle that level of ability you will at least have an image of where you can be sometime in the future.

Positive People - Focus on people who believe in you and who believe you can succeed especially if they are experienced in the area you are tackling. Forget about people who usually, without even realizing it, out of their own failure and need to convince themselves something is not possible try to convince you too that you won't succeed as well. Misery loves company as they say.

Balance - Take a break from whatever area you are focusing on. With exploring different parts of life, you will likely realize that the area you are focused on is not the end and beginning of your life. This alone will make you more relaxed, confident and allow you to see the bigger picture making it easier to avoid the so called 'tunnel vision'.

Following the first five steps and repeating them in a cycle will slowly but surely start to bring some real results with your fears going away being replaced by more and more confidence in your own ability to master not only the area of your choosing but pretty much anything that life can throw out at you! Once you have proven to yourself and started believing that you can succeed in something there is no reason that you can't succeed at anything else.

There is no greater gift in life than having the heart of a lion. The belief in yourself and proving to yourself that you can have realistic, achievable dreams and are able to bring them to reality!

ACTION & BOLDNESS

Thoughts define reality, words put it into motion but it is the actions that create it

If there is one obvious truth that everyone seems to acknowledge but yet few seem to live by, it is the fact that everyone around us prefers to talk instead of take action. We have all been there and done that, made detailed plans of our future but failed to put any of that into reality. On one end I get it, it is so much easier and cheaper to weave stories and make promises instead of actually doing some real work and this will even get us some quick wins. On the other end, we should all ask ourselves the question if that's really the best we can do? Probably not.

When I was younger and hopefully less wise, I used to talk a lot more about everything instead of actually doing it. Grandiose plans and dreams that were too far into the future and waiting for all the right circumstances. While it is good to have goals and dreams and share them at some stage with the people that surround us, there is a point where it becomes unproductive if not done in the right way. So let me follow my own advice, stop writing about it and see what we can actually DO about it?

People - Surround yourself with people who have the same philosophy and approach, so called Doers instead of Talkers.

Talking - Some kind of communication is necessary with any kind of action. The question we need to ask ourselves is at what stage further talk becomes unproductive.

Simple - Instead of making the absolute master plan first and putting it into motion, try to think of the absolute minimum planning before you can put things into action. Don't fall into the trap of wanting to do something but 'only if...'. There is no excuse for taking the first step.

Reflection - Once you have started taking action, make sure to analyze the results and go back to the drawing board as soon as possible. Always remember that reality is the best planner, you never know how things work until you actually try.

Celebrate - One of the most underestimated point. Make sure to celebrate and reward yourself and your accomplices for any positive result from your actions. If celebrating was not necessary, champions wouldn't do it.

Boldness - Taking action is not enough. You need to take action with boldness to ensure its success. Whatever bold action you take and fail, fear not, it can probably be fixed by yet another bold action.

Baby Steps - Failing a baby step and getting up hurts a lot less than jumping from the plane and having the parachute not open. Take action but do it so in a controlled and steady way where you can always fall back if needed. Take huge risks only when absolutely necessary

The beauty about mastering action over talking is that it provides you additional ways of viewing the world and the people that surround you. Suddenly you learn to look beyond all the words that especially in our modern age seem to have gotten cheaper and easily broken. You learn to know the real value of people simply by forgetting what they say and looking ONLY at what they actually DO.

FIRST CLASS FUTURE

You can never hope to receive that which you are not willing to wholeheartedly give

Have you ever asked yourself why is it that certain things in life are so far out of our reach that they are almost in the realm of fantasy, like a luxury boat? Even more importantly, what is the common attribute of these luxury things that make them so expensive and so highly desired? The answer is very simple, superior quality. But what does it actually mean having superior quality and how do we achieve it in our own lives? Having a luxury yacht is pretty nice but have you ever thought about quality in a deeper sense of the word as in quality of your entire life for everything that it stands for?

It may seem counterintuitive, but you don't need to sacrifice your efforts or costs or pay large amounts of money in order to get top quality for most of what life has to offer. The biggest mistake most people make when it comes to quality in general is that they forget about having reciprocity or expanding this concept to their entire life. If you want a first-class lifestyle, you need to focus on providing first class value to others. You need to focus on the best and deepest of what life has to offer in every single moment and every single area, making this a life philosophy.

"I have offended God and mankind because my work didn't reach the quality it should have" - Leonardo da Vinci

It is unfortunate and really sad that so much in our world today is driven by instant gratification, quick fixes, cheap merchandise and short-term profit at the expense of long term sustainability. Every time I go out in the city to buy myself some new shoes, there is an old saying that I always remember that goes: "I am not that rich to buy cheap shoes". Now every time I DO buy some cheap shoes because I really like them, I always make sure to keep the receipt because usually within few months they fall apart and then I have to return them and get a new pair :). There is a bright side to all this however. In these days where quality has become such a rare commodity, it has become easier to stand out among the rest even with mediocre efforts and products.

You don't have to be a factory or company owner in order to focus on top quality. Remember that this is a mindset and a life philosophy, not an Excel table where you shift costs vs. quality of results and products. When is the last time you thought about the quality of the conversation with your best friend? When is the last time you thought about what defines a 'good' friend? When is the last time you considered the quality of how you spend your day?

How much time did you spend on watching commercial breaks advertising cheap worthless products and how much time was spent by doing something that touches you deep within your soul or produces some deep value for someone else?

Let's see how you can provide top quality to others and make them feel first class through four key concepts, because you can never hope to receive that which you are not willing to wholeheartedly give first.

Focus on sustainability and longevity. Analyze all the situations in which people receive value from you. This includes work, family and friends. Is the value you provide focused on short term gains at the expense of long term sustainability? Do your relationships on and off work have depth, meaning and last for years or are they based on more superficial short term values?

Provide people what they really need, not what they want in the moment based on their mood or even worse only what you are required to give them. When Steve Jobs was asked about market research, his answer was that it is useless because people did not know yet what they really need.

Seek reciprocity in all relationships. Do not be afraid to ask the right price for your superior quality and by this I don't mean only money. Surround yourself with the best people (work and friends) and make sure they do not take your relationship for granted

Give with higher purpose and deeper meaning. Focusing on the first three concepts will create a positive spiral of ever increasing quality, deeper relationships and increasing reciprocity. Ultimately this leads to unique values that very few others can provide. Values that have their higher purpose and deeper meaning.

There are no shortcuts here. Nobody becomes a first-class star and the king of the castle overnight. Even those born into royalty in the old times, sooner or later had to prove their worth. It is a long process of growth, deepening relationships and continual increase of the quality of your values during the process.

Applying these concepts and making quality as part of your life philosophy will slowly start to change not only the perception of others towards you, not only will they start providing you more value, trust and investment in you but the most important of all, you will start to respect who you are and will never settle for anything less but the best of what life has to offer.

TOP PERFORMANCE

> *I couldn't find the sports car of my dreams, so I built it myself. —*
> *Ferdinand Porsche*

Few years ago, I had the opportunity to visit the Porsche museum in Stuttgart during my vacation in Germany. For some reason, I had always been a huge fan of the Porsche brand. Sure, they are not the fastest cars on the market but there is a certain simplicity and beauty that I feel drawn to. What fascinates me most about Porsche is the mindset, the elegance and their ability to extract the optimal performance without any excessive waste. I believe that's a lesson we can all learn from and apply to our lives.

What can we do to extract the maximum we can from any project in our lives, personal or professional and unlock the secrets to performance? As Ferdinand Porsche would say: "A good idea is often surprisingly simple."

It is fairly unfortunate that even after thousands of years of evolution we still live in a 'quick fix - magic bullet' oriented society. There are far too many expectations that a holy grail or a hero will suddenly appear, wash all the problems away and catapult us to a whole new level practically overnight. Sure, one in a billion occasionally wins the lottery but that is just the exception proving the rule. There are no miracles when it comes to achieving the maximum performance that you are capable of, only smart work and time. The idea behind it may be simple but it still requires that we put the work in it. We all have areas in our lives where we are not performing well. The highway to performance has several stops on it, choose an area where you are not performing well and let's take a short trip:

Strengths vs. Weaknesses - Make a list of the strengths and weaknesses in that area.

Detail - Do not underestimate even the smallest detail. Even if you save only few seconds or dollars on a certain task, this could add up to years or millions if you are performing this task every hour until the end of your life. I often give the example on my courses about learning to type with all 10 fingers. It practically saves you 3-4 years of your life after you make the calculation.

Practice - Invest time to practice and optimize any skills that are affecting your performance. You can achieve amazing feats if you put the hours into practicing your skills.

Design & Outsource - You can't be a master in everything. See about the options of giving a small part of your activities to someone else. Porsche may be the designer of their cars but a lot of the small parts of their cars are made by other companies.

Dead Weight - Sooner or later a certain area of your project or life drains more energy than it provides you, be it money, emotions or time. Identify those areas or even people and make sure to either transform them into a more balanced relationship or cut them off. IBM is a very good example of that with either transforming or selling off divisions when the profits get too low.

Passion - You can never be at the top of your game and performance if you are not passionate about what you are doing. Either find new ways on how to be excited about what you are doing or focus your energy in other areas.

Porsche - was not built in a day and neither can you achieve high levels of performance in a short amount of time. Know when to give up but also know when to remain persistent at all cost. By persistence alone you will usually outperform the most of your competition but even more importantly yourself.

Full Package - Remember that it is always about the whole package. If you are low performing in one area it has the danger of having a chain reaction to your entire life and other high performing areas. How would a brand-new Porsche 911 run with old worn out tires? Not very well I would assume. Go back to point 5 and make the hard decisions.

If at any time you feel like there is something preventing you from being at the maximum of your possible performance or that you are missing something important, realize that it is an illusion. There is no possible excuse that you can make for not giving 100% of yourself to something you care for. If something is missing, go and find it or create it yourself! Low performance is always a choice due to a lack of motivation or lack of belief in your own self. Move up or move on, there are no sideways when it comes to performance and there is no sweeter reward at the end, than being at the top of your game. Bon Appetite!

PERCEPTION IS GOLDEN

It's not what we don't know that surprises us the most but what we thought we knew

As we grow older and gain more experience, we tend to judge people and situations more quickly. This is sometimes to our advantage as it allows us to make decisions faster but at other times it can blind us and we miss to see the real potential that has been, sometimes literally for years, right in front of our eyes. What can we do to avoid this self-inflicted limitation and see the world around us with all the potential that it has?

In the earlier chapters I described how surprising it was to discover that skiing is such a great sport but it does not compare to my re-discovery and surprise as to just how much I still enjoy dancing as well even though I thought I had experienced the best it had to offer. There will be no step by step guides in this chapter.

Back in 2002 was the year when I first started dancing. It was a great adventure that lead me from one experience to another, met some great people, did some shows together and by the summer of 2003 I had decided it was time to move on to more 'serious' things, like figuring out what I was going to do for a living after my studies. It's probably no secret that I like to venture in all styles of dancing, including the so-called Aerobics which immediately to most people brings pictures of girls in spandex jumping around including few guys - also in spandex. Well, let's just say that quite a few things have changed since the 80s. Fast forward to 2010. Out of boredom I and a friend decided to pay a visit to a local gym where IBM has a good deal. I felt more like a tourist than anything else as at that time the heaviest thing I had lifted for few years were my weekly grocery bags. After lifting a few very light weights boredom started to set in and he started looking around the gym.

"Hey, look at this, they have a lot of Aerobics classes, we should try one." He proclaimed confidently with a straight face.

"Did you bring your spandex suit?" I quipped at him and immediately burst into laughter.

"What do we have to lose?" He insisted without giving a single laugh at my total unbelief.

"Well, how about our sanity? Haven't you seen Jane Fonda and the 80s superhero spandex squad around her?" I just couldn't get the image out of my head of those 80s guys with mustaches literally jumping all over the stage in full body spandex suits.

"But look, one of the classes is led by a guy named Tomas, it can't be THAT crazy if his name is Tomas, right?" He kept on pushing for reasons I will never understand because after he convinced me for the first class he never came with me again. Too physically demanding was his repeating excuse for the years to come.

"Ok, whatever dude, let's go next time but we go to that guy Tomas' class to make sure we are not the only crazy creepy guys there" – I gave in mostly out of curiosity and partly out of wanting to try something completely new that was as far out of my comfort zone as it can get at the time.

As I mentioned, things have changed since the 80's. Even though it was only partly a dance class the mere rhythm and simple choreographies brought back nice memories from the dance years I thought I had forever put behind. One class after another I started going for the real dance classes which had almost nothing in common with the regular ones. While I was at it I even became a certified Aerobics instructor for which I had to listen to a metronome 10 hours a day to make sure I get the eight beats rhythm down to my bones. I still haven't taught a single class to this day but if I love doing something, I like mastering the basics first so I don't have to think about them anymore and fully enjoy the moment.

As I further explored my limits the next step was to join a dance crew – Magic Free Group Brno. In the age category where I unfortunately belong we did not have that much serious competition so we went on to win bronze, silver, golden medals all over Czech Republic and did some exhibition shows like dancing for Miss Brno 2012. I probably have over 10 of those. I do not mean to brag or anything as we all mainly did it for the incredible fun and excitement of dancing in front of a screaming audience of thousands but the main point was that with having experienced and 'achieved' all this I thought it was time to leave dancing behind and focus on other things. I left the dance crew and as my career needed a lot of focus at that time it was probably a good choice on some level to limit my dancing to as low as maybe once in three months where I went to regular dance aerobics classes just to remind myself of some nice old memories. Naturally with so much on my mind and low practice I was not doing a very good job and not enjoying it as much as I used to.

End of the summer 2014 something surprising happened. I found a different way on how to look at the world and people around me thanks to a few dance aerobics classes. We spend so much time analyzing the past, thinking of where we are and how it is going to affect our future that it overwhelms us and locks us down from making the right choices and making those adjustments to the sails that our hearts tell us to make. I decided that once the music starts that I would stop thinking about the outside world and fully immerse myself into the magic of it all sharing it with the people around me. Not only had I rediscovered my love for dancing but most importantly I had finally figured out the main reason why I had always loved it so much. It is because to fully enjoy a dance and do it properly you can't think too much of the previous or future steps and you must fully focus only on the moment and feel the music covering it all only with a very faint feeling about the next step.

I am always reminded of that realization and it always makes me smile when my favorite dance instructor always says to relax if we make any mistakes and take it easy that we are not at a competition. Interestingly enough I tend to enjoy a dance routine with no mistakes a whole lot more when I don't have to beat anyone for a piece of metal and the only thing I am free to focus on is the infinite amount of moments that a dance choreography as short as 2 minutes has and share them with the people around me.

SUCCESS

I was recently asked to define success in my life and what it means to me. Sure, I have won some shiny trinkets with pieces of paper but overall, failure has been much more common in my life than one would assume by looking at those shiny trinkets. It really got me thinking as to why projects and even sometimes people are marked as a failure. In most of those cases where I had gone back and investigated it was very interesting to see that it was usually not because of a lack of skills or shortcomings on the side of the person but simply because there was no clear definition of the success criteria. Quite often a lot of good work was done but simply in the wrong direction or under the wrong assumption. Naturally this often results into huge frustrations as the person feels unappreciated that even after all the effort, they put the recognition never came.

Few years ago, I had just taken over a very troubled project from another manager that was doing a pretty good job but was not very good with communicating with senior management so he was promptly expedited to take on 'other challenges'. As this was the third failed Project Manager in a row on this project, I knew I had to pull out a rabbit out of a hat or suffer the same fate. As I fixed all the obvious shortcomings of my unfortunate predecessors, I felt that the negative aura around the project still remained and people were still not satisfied with how things were going. The team was working very efficiently, delivering regularly, communicating properly all the way up and failing only where it was stopped by other external factors outside of our control. My thinking at the time was that as long as we commit very aggressive targets, work real hard and show this to our sponsors that we would be appreciated and recognized for it. Right? … Wrong!

Our sponsors were annoyed that we were failing behind our targets, even though they were very aggressive to begin with and usually not due to our fault. The fact that at the same time I was leading another project which I also took over with unrealistic targets and ended up getting escalated all over the place also didn't help very much with my mental and emotional well-being. It was time to go back to the drawing board on both projects. I managed to negotiate new targets with the sponsors which were moderately aggressive and at the same time agreed with the team internally that we will push for 20% higher than what was negotiated externally in order to cover for all the failed ones caused by external factors. By establishing new success criteria, suddenly we became a 'success story' and received one praise after another for regularly beating the targets and finishing the project without any delays. We went from zero to hero practically overnight. Long story short, not only did we recover from a potentially career damaging situation, but I even went on to get second place on the Brno Project of the Year, beaten only by another monster of a project that I had also led. Yup. Speaking about the toughest competition being yourself. A huge turnaround caused by one single action, negotiating clear and realistic success criteria.

Sometimes though, we fail even though the criteria were realistic and well established. I have noticed very recently that in such cases it is usually because of self-limiting beliefs, fear and prejudice. I was doing pretty poorly in some areas of my life and as I started digging deeper to find the reasons behind it, I realized one simple thing. My mindset and the way I was approaching the problems in this area was completely different than what I was doing in areas of life where I was having great success. I wrongly assumed that different areas should have different mindsets and attitudes. My next step was to take the mindset of the successful areas and apply it to the ones where I was lacking. At first it felt really strange, uncomfortable and downright scary but I did not have to wait long for some major breakthroughs and successes to start pouring in. Naturally this only encouraged me to take even bolder steps that brought even higher gains.

Have you ever considered taking your successful mindset and attitude from one area of life to another? Give it a try and let me know

111

when it starts bringing results for you as well.

Success means many different things to many different people, but one thing is the same for everyone. We all know how horrible it feels to fail and at the same time how alive we feel when we finally succeed. Most of us already have the answers to a successful project or life within us, if we only gather the courage to look within, we may just find that missing piece that causes all the stars to finally align for us.

We may not win the world cup, but I firmly believe we can all take action, achieve success and feel like a champion in the areas of life that matter the most to us.

FINANCIAL DEATH BY A THOUSAND CUTS

Sometimes, the best deals are those you don't make! — 45ᵗʰ US President

Sign up to receive this special financial death by a thousand cuts. It doesn't sound too appealing, does it? You would never wish that even upon your worst enemies? That's why companies rather go with something a whole lot nicer.

"Get our service (without SIM) for only 60 EUR per month and you will have a new mid-model iPhone every 2 years! or pay an additional 10 EUR to get the high-end model! If you sign for the 5-year plan, you get a 20% discount!"

Some of you might be wondering what sort of a person would fall for something like that? Well. that sort of a person is actually my brother. He typically goes for deals like that and anytime I try to convince him to the utter financial nonsense of the deal his simple is answer is: "It is just 70 EUR per month (he works in Italy), I will barely feel it".

There are two dangers of the modern business model which is spiraling completely out of control ruining the lives of thousands of people. There have been 792 thousand warrants for seizure of property due to unpaid loans and financial obligations in the Czech Republic in 2016 alone! That is one warrant per 13 people!

1. Services based businesses
2. Micro-transactions

Let's have a look where you can find both and some effective tactics to avoid them or even turn them to work in your favor.

Services based businesses

They provide comfort (or so they say), flexibility (unless you sign a 3-year contract), small down payment, less risk and saving of your time by taking away the burden of ownership.

"Hmm.. well it sounds pretty good, why should I not use them??"

The only way to answer that question is to start counting. We are not going to get smarter with our finances without at least a bit of math so bear with me please:

Always calculate the price of the service per 2 years. Why 2 years? Because products usually have a 2-year warranty and you will need to compare this price to owning a product risk free.

The service for the new iPhone will cost you 70EUR * 24months = 1680 EUR (prices based on an actual offer in Brno/CZ). After the contract is over, there is no left-over value... ZERO.

Sum total = -1680 EUR ... oops, it doesn't look anymore so appealing as 70 EUR.

Now compare that with the price of a new product (or as close as you can get to the new one). The same iPhone bought as a stand-alone product = 787 EUR. In 2 years, electronics usually loses about 20% of value per year these days. So, the iPhone in 2 years can be sold for about 500 EUR.

Sum total = 787 - 500 = -287 EUR.

"But hold on, with the service I am care free.. I don't have to buy or sell phones etc etc"

I get it... That's why in Project Management we also count the work effort that comes with the options. Let's say the work effort required from your side will be about 3 hours more with the option B. Posting some adds, finding buyers etc.

The difference between both options is a whopping 1393. Unless you are making 500 EUR per hour and your time is so precious then I would really suggest you go for the second option.

Still. There is an extreme amount of people who will never go with the second option simply because of the fact that they don't have the cash on hand to buy such an expensive phone... but they do have just enough cash to pay the next monthly charge... which pretty much ensures they will never ever save enough for a new phone.. which service companies love.

In such a case I can only advise that you maybe take a couple of steps back, get used to a humbler way of life until you save some cash that will open many options of being more efficient with your spending as most of the time you get discounts for putting cash up front (example a yearly public transport ticket or a 40 entry gym card). There are many other ways to enjoy life even without owning the newest Macbook Air, Audi A5 or iPhone 7.

Of course, in many cases using services is an excellent idea as it allows for specialization and efficiency. Every time I go into a restaurant, I am using a service because obviously buying and owning a restaurant and inviting a bunch for people for the social setting would be far more expensive :). Renting a flat is also a service that for many situations is far more efficient than owning a flat. For example if I am on a one year assignment or plan to move. I am also not going to buy a power-plant but will gladly use electricity as a service.

All I am saying is to do your math before you go one way or the other.

Micro-transactions

Have you played any smartphone games lately? You were doing SO WELL in the game, totally blasting it but then somehow the game got progressively harder and harder. Fear not... all you need to do is to buy a few magic crystals for 2 EUR to ease your pain. It is just 2 EUR... who cares, right? WRONG. There are people who are literally addicted and spending north of 1000 EUR per month on certain video games.

League of Legends made a whopping 500 million EUR only by using a micro transactions model! Micro-transactions use a relatively crude but very efficient psychological model to rip you off. They employ several psychological manipulative tricks to do so:

Draw and attach you emotionally by offering you sign-up rewards, free to play time and various feel good mechanisms.

Cause you pain by slowing down your progress and rewards you get

Compare you to other people on your level and the fact you are failing behind

Offer you the remedy and cure in the form of a small micro-transaction pain killer that will cost you 'almost nothing'

Repeat the process

Video games are not your thing? How about a cup of coffee from the coffee bar... it is only 2 EUR! It will cost you 'almost nothing' and you will feel so much better... plus everybody is having a cup of coffee you need one too! Or maybe a cigarette?

Getting a coffee from the bar once in a while is a nice social experience but if you are a daily user, you might want to calculate how much is your small 'harmless' habit costing you per year. Most people I talk to are either absolutely shocked at the amount or try to avoid the subject all-together as they feel it will be a painful one (usually chronic smokers).

Turning the Tables

The business models above are mainly based on psychology. They use your own subconscious mechanisms against you. Humans are not really well built to recognize 4 dimensional dangers. Our brains are wired to react to the nearest and most immediate dangers. So a 5 EUR charge will not be registered by our brain as something important or dangerous. But a 3650 EUR charge will give you a heart attack (the second amount is how much you end up paying only in 2 years because of a 'harmless' habit that costs you 5 EUR per day).

"Marty , you are not thinking 4th dimensionally!"

Two powerful tips and actions to take at the end:

Use contactless forms of payment and online payments! These days you can pay with contactless card almost everywhere. The primary reason is that every single transaction will be logged in your card statement.

After 3 months you can sit down, transfer it all in excel, find your biggest spending habits or any recurring services-based charges you might have forgotten about and calculate how much they cost you per 2 years.

Disclaimer: I won't be held responsible for any heart attacks resulting from this exercise! :D

Oh yea. And the cherry on the top is that banks will usually pay you 1% of your whole spending (back in cash immediately the following month) if you use a credit card! Provided you are psychologically restrained enough to top off your credit card at the end of each month. Can be automated of course.

Not only you don't have to bother with coins, paper etc, not only you get a powerful analytical excel table, but they actually pay you to do it :). Not to mention it is a huge time saver.

There are of course many other financial hacks I have under my sleeve but the top two are the ones that have the most extreme impact to people that decide to turn the tables on them.

DEALS – LEVERAGE IS EVERYTHING

Love may influence hearts and minds, but it is leverage that permanently changes them

I am appalled as to how many people fall for bad deals and fall under the spell of second grade sales using few common manipulation techniques. A month later they realize just how awful deal they made and unleash on the internet a barrage of bad sentiment towards the company that sold them something.

I come from the Balkans where haggling is part of life and it is usually quite uncommon to get something at the price originally advertised, unless of course you are buying some cheese at an international supermarket chain. The good news is that most prices even in 1st world countries are negotiable. A rule of thumb - The larger the price, the more room for negotiation. Even when I bought a used bicycle the first thing, I did was to outright send 5 e-mail to 5 sellers offering them a price which was 20% lower than the one advertised. Huge surprise... NOT ... all of them replied and agreed. One of them countered with 15% discount and she got the deal, mainly because the original price of the bike was much higher.

Few years back I used several techniques to get a really nice deal on a used Hyundai i30 (chapter Intent) including the best deal possible on the full insurance package which I successfully re-negotiated this summer for a 20% discount, simply by not trusting the automatic re-newal process and asking them point-blank to re-calculate me their newest best deal.

Few months later I needed to get another major product and once again the techniques described in one of the previous chapters worked like a charm. Once again, I did my research, found all the reviews of bitter people who did a lousy job negotiating, contacted the top 2 companies in the industry, got a meeting with them and asked them my favorite question which always catches them by surprise. I just love the shocked expression on their face as for some reason very few peo-ple like to be as direct.

Let's call them Company Pit Bull and Company Underdog.

"Company Underdog is your key competitor, I will be honest with you, I have a meeting with them in an hour. Why should I choose you? How are you better than Company Underdog?"

I ask the same question even if this is the second meeting. Why give out the fact that I have already met the competition and already have their offer?

Situation: I had two meetings lined up in the same day, through reference of someone else directly with the team leaders of the sales department of both companies.Let's see how the meetings went, what mistakes they made and how you should avoid making the same mistakes with your clients:

Company Underdog:

Meeting scheduled at 15:00:

Arrived - no reception at the premise. I had to ask around busy people how to find Person X.

Mistake number 1: No clear instructions for the meeting and how to find Person X.

Once I met Person X I realized she is subordinate to the team leader that I was originally in contact with.

Mistake number 2: Delegating me to your subordinates is not going to make me feel good. The very least you should greet me in the first 5 minutes and then delegate me. Person X told me that she is awfully sorry but that I should wait until she finishes her previous meeting.

Mistake number 3: Never ever make a customer wait for 30

minutes when you have scheduled a specific time for the meeting. Especially your first meeting. After some talk about the bottom line and price I got to ask my favorite question. How are you better than Company Pit Bull.

"Well, we take special interest in our customers. You will always have priority access to our staff in case you have any problems with our product." Followed by waiting 10 minutes as their system hung up.

Mistake number 4: BZZZZ .. Wrong answer! .. if priority access means getting delegated to you, waiting 30 minutes to meet you and then getting an answer that is absolutely out of touch with the reality of your company, all while your system crashed in the middle of a common form filling, then I can't even begin to imagine what does normal access mean to you.I am going now to meet company Pit Bull , can you make me a better offer.

"We are going to make you an offer that is the same as company Pit Bull"

Mistake number 5: If you are going to make an offer, always try to make it better than your competition. Especially if your client service was horrible and especially if you are the underdog.

Company Pit Bull:

Scheduled time: 16:00

Arrived at the reception, gave my name, was promptly told to go upstairs. 30 seconds later I am sitting in a comfortable room with the team lead of the sales department even though there are several regular sales people available at the premises.

Good move 1: Taking personal interest and investing the busy schedule of a team lead, especially at a top company is always a good sign.

After discussing the bottom line (which is already better than company Underdog) I get to ask my favorite question:

How are you better than Company Underdog?

Answer (given in very self-confident way): "We are the biggest and best on the market and can offer the best prices"

Good move 2: I dislike fake humbleness and I like healthy self-confidence, especially when people have the courage to say they are the best and biggest. I don't trust it yet, but that's what the next meetings should prove right or wrong.

"Listen, I have a meeting with Company Underdog, what if they provide me better bottom line?" (I already had the offer in my bag but pretended I didn't.)

"Well, they are our key competitor, in such case please send it to me and I will be interested to have a look at it. Also keep in mind that on the second item of the package we have a 20% advantage. All in all, I don't believe they are able to provide a better quote."

Good move 3: The team lead is very frank with me (probably recognizing I am no push-over myself and would not fall for any cheap talk in the form of 'priority access'). I am also impressed with the detailed knowledge of their key competitors.

Second round of negotiations:

Meanwhile company Underdog keeps calling me on my cell phone every couple of days asking me if I will buy from them:

Mistake number .. #I lost count... We live in the digital age. Grow up please. You have my e-mail, send me a message. Calling someone without prior schedule borders on rudeness. The very least you can send me an SMS. Especially when I gave you my promise that I will contact YOU when I am ready.

No unnecessary calls from company Pit Bull .. communication is on-going through e-mail.

I take the quote from Pit Bull and send it over to Underdog telling them to quote me the best final offer. After a couple of days for waiting for approval from head quarters, they get back to me with a quote that is basically the same as company Pit Bull.

Mistake number.. # too many.. You messed up all the client relationship stuff and the best you can do is getting me the same bottom line? Thank you but no thank you.

My fiancée at this stage tells me I seem to be enjoying this, that this is not a sport but business and that I should probably get it done :). I tell her I am not finished yet :)

I open excel, crunch the numbers and realize that the offer of Pit Bull is ever slightly better, plus the better customer service convinces me I am going with them even if they can't give me anything lower. But I am not showing my cards yet. Quite the opposite I try to appear as if though I am leaning towards Underdog.

I get the final offer from Underdog and send it over to Pit Bull and ask them if they can do better that this. Pit Bull also asks for corporate headquarters approval and gets me a deal that is about 5% better than their original deal plus a couple of free perks here and there. I just love leverage :). I send an e-mail to Underdog telling them I am going with Pit Bull and thanking them for their effort and time. Underdog calls me two weeks later asking me if I have really gone with Pit Bull.

Mistake #facepalm: Try to use e-mail please. I realize some people don't answer you, but I have given you every indication this is my preferred and reliable form of communication.

Final round:

The whole process is expressly finished at the next live meeting by the professionals at Pit Bull with very clear instructions. Once again, I am not delegated but taken directly by the team lead. I leave the final meeting feeling I have been taken care of and am an important customer to them. The feeling for company Underdog? Well ... I think #facepalm should suffice.

TEACHING – A TWO WAY STREET

*If you want to perfect something, teach it. If you want to under-
stand people perfectly, teach them*

Have you ever thought about mentoring someone? Maybe even construct your own presentation or workshop? Due to changing organizational priorities I will be putting my teaching side-career on the back burner for the foreseeable future so this seems to be the perfect opportunity, after spending many years actively teaching, to share all the reasons why it is a great idea to take once you are an 'expert' in your field.

Back in 2012 after making several presentations my colleagues recommended that I start teaching. That was as crazy sounding to me as if you would tell Michael Jordan to play Soccer as I absolutely hated most of the education process in my life with the very few exceptions of excellent teachers along the way. But I said yes, because finally I had the chance to 'do it right' and 'do it my way'.

Fast forward 2017, after delivering over 100 workshops for

international audiences of over 3000 people in IBM, Universities, Conferences etc etc. it is time to look back and see what I learnt from the process.

You change people's lives profoundly - The side benefits are good for teaching but nothing really makes your day such as receiving an e-mail from a person you have totally forgotten (it is tough to remember hundreds of people per year) telling you that the advice you gave them 2 years ago has landed them in a great place today. Thankfully I haven't received any e-mails ... yet ... blaming me that my advice destroyed their career... :D

Teaching others makes you an excellent communicator - You think other people understand what you just said until you ask them to repeat it. You never really get to see just how difficult is to share a very simple message to 20 people until you have them take a test after it. It took me 3 years of active teaching to refine my communication skill on a level where 90% of the room understood what I wanted them to understand. The 10%? Still lost in the woods beyond any help ;)

People are afraid to confront authority - I always begin the workshop by inviting for comments and especially different and conflicting points of view to promote diversity of thought. How many people actually confront me on something I say? I would say about three percent. Always invite confrontations in life, especially if you are literally 'on the spot' in front of 25 people. It has greatly strengthened my confidence... and ability to brainstorm a plausible explanation if things are burning under my feet :)

You understand the education industry with all its positives and flaws - The education system of today is broken. Companies sell workshops to make money, not to teach you. The longer it takes, the better, and more expensive for you. Teachers are the prisoners of satisfaction surveys. Their goal is not to teach you but to make sure you give them the best satisfaction rating you can possibly give them because their benefits are directly tied to that survey. We all have that one tough teacher we hated in high school but totally grew to be grateful for the tough times they gave us because it taught us so much. Such a teacher would get abysmal satisfaction scores today and would be out of a job in a month. I had to play the same game... to a degree... I assume telling some people to shut up or leave is not the best strategy for sat scores ;)

You develop your presentation skills beyond what you thought possible - You may think you are a great presenter until you have clocked over 1000 hours of presenting in front of live audiences. Even after my first 1000 hours I still discover new ways to make the experience better and grab attention more effectively... Nothing works quite as well as showing them a photo of my dance history with messed up hair... Attention guaranteed ;)

You become immune to criticism - In the last one year it has become a trending anonymous feedback that out of 10 people at least one or two would write me that it has been the best workshop they have ever had with the best teacher they have ever had. Hold on .. I am not boasting ... because one in about 50-100 people on the other hand would write me that they were not satisfied with the workshop and that the teacher was arrogant (I am a little bit, yes .. surprisingly :)). After the math is done, I forget about that unhappy person. "Sorry guy/girl No. 2143 that you didn't enjoy my workshop last month. Nobody cares. The previous 100 people did."

You realize you were not a true expert - You think you are an expert in something until you try to teach it to others, see how it is received and face tough conflicting questions on the spot. After delivering the very same 8-hour workshop for the 70th time and fine-tuning it every time to make it more understandable than the last one, you start seeing matters on a very deep level and new connections appear that suddenly make everything much clearer. These days I could probably explain IT project management even to my grandmother :)

Networking and insight in your area of expertise - You make literally thousands of contacts that you probably forget but due to the direct interaction and feedback during the workshops your insight into your area of expertise grows and you grow to understand the big difference between the theory in your field and the way it is practiced on the ground. This is probably the greatest benefit my teaching has brought me. I am able to forecast very accurately how is a new process or method going to be accepted by the community of project management and with what kind of a success rate. Executives don't love me for telling them their programs/tools/processes will fail if I am asked for a review, but I do try to avoid telling them 'I told you so' a year later if they don't listen ;)

The last lesson, perhaps the most powerful is the lesson of humility. By teaching actively you truly come to understand that a true teacher never stops to learn. One of the most surprising feedback I got in the last few months was that I am a humble teacher. Either that person was hallucinating or the 100+ workshops have truly made me a humbler person. I probably still have some learning to do in this area to reach the level of a certain US president who once said:

"I am by far the humblest person on the face of the Earth! You'd be shocked at the degree to which I'm humble. No one even comes close!"

AWARENESS IS EVERYTHING

Professionalism without awareness is foolishness. It won't do you any good to be the best violin player on the Titanic

When I was 10 years old, the most boring thing in the world I could possibly imagine was when my grandfather would switch the TV to the National Channel No.1 at 19:30 every day so he can watch the news. As we didn't have another TV so I could watch the only remaining option National Channel No.2, I quickly left the room to go read some comics or computer magazines. Later on, I would rather play games on my Commodore 64.

Little did I know that our dear country Yugoslavia was falling apart with war looming behind the corner and that my classes of Russian language in primary school were probably not going to be very useful in a world where the Soviet Union would be no more. My grandfather watched the news every single day, but he never really saw it coming. Very few people did. We avoided the war in Macedonia, but we didn't avoid the economic downfall that keeps spiraling out of control up to this day.

I consider myself more lucky than smart in those years that my inner desire was to leave the country at all cost combined with a passion for computers. I still remember people and kids from the village pretty much laughing at me for playing with my computers or arcade games all day when clearly those expensive toys were never going to help me put food on the table... Clearly... "You can't even drive a Tractor" - They said. My favorite TV Show of the time? "Beyond the year 2000" & "Star Trek TNG". Their favorite TV Show? Yugoslavian TV novels and later on a soap opera from Venezuela called "Cassandra". Well ok, Cassandra was not that bad really :)

My other favorite subject at the time was physics. One of the first dreams I had, like every other nerdy child, was to build a perpetuum mobile. A machine that produces endless energy without using any resources. Then one day I learned about the laws of thermodynamics and the conservation of energy. For something to gain energy, something else has to radiate it. Zero Point energy you say? Even if it is real, what is to say that it is not sucking the energy out of some other less fortunate universe?

In business we just love the mantra 'Win - Win' solutions... yet when we look at world politics and dynamics for the last 5000 years, we can very clearly see a Win - Lose dynamic of wealth exchanging hands. Sometimes it is voluntary through money, other times it takes some smart politics and when politics don't work out, there is always war to clear up any misunderstandings.

How do you thrive in such a world?

Follow the money - Step away from the emotional TV novels and daily gaffes of leading politicians. Those are high on emotion, very low on actual substance. Understand true intentions and shifts of power by following the self-interest and money of the leading global players & special interests behind them.

Invest your life in the successful politically - economic countries. If you don't understand the global shifts of power, you are shooting blind. No matter my talents, had I stayed in Macedonia, chances are I would be a taxi driver by now.

Invest in capital and yourself - If you have chosen well, investing in some capital in a growing area will bring you some passive wealth. If you have chosen poorly chances are you will never quite catch up only based on your skills. In either way, an investment in your skills will go a long way towards either offsetting or enhancing your capital investments.

Top 3 Skills to invest at

1. Financial awareness. Start looking at money as score-keeping for Personal Power. "Money is Evil" is a slogan designed to keep the powerless without power.

2. Soft Skills (Negotiation, Communication, Social Dynamics)

3. Any specialist skill (IT, Medicine, Construction) - whatever your passion and wherever the economic trends are going.

Make a decision and pick a side - Once you learn about the major sides of the world, chances are your personal situation & philosophy will either lean you to the so called left, or the so called right. Make a decision. Remember that those stuck in the middle are on the front lines in between two armies. Unless you are rich as Switzerland and you can buy your neutrality, chances are you will be caught in the crossfire, or worse, completely ignored.

Vote in elections - Let's face it, your single vote is mathematically in the realm of voting error and will not change anything whatsoever. I also am not in favor of treating it as a duty. The freedom of thought also means you are free to delegate your life priorities to the majority of voters. The key reason to vote is a psychological anchor that will help you:

1. Establish your values in life

2. Create a life philosophy towards solving the biggest problems of humanity

3. Prioritize your resources and choices

Prepare for the future, not the past - Any investor will tell you that past success does not predict future success. For this reason alone, you should always:

1. Stay in touch with the developing world trends
2. Be aware of the Gartner's Hype Curve to avoid any hype traps. (Bitcoin anyone?)
3. Invest in capital and skills that will be relevant in the future

Ask for inspiration from multiple sources and don't rely on the power of authority.

When I was a child, I received two life lessons; one from my grandfather who was a financial director in communist Yugoslavia and another from my uncle, who was an engineer in a local mine.

My grandfather heavily criticized me for having weird ideas out of the norm and told me to simply do what everyone else is doing. My uncle looking at me simply told me I don't belong in the village where I was born. Years later my grandfather changed his mind as Yugoslavia collapsed but it was my uncle who was the first one to see my future. They both taught me a powerful lesson.

Don't let anyone else tell you how to live your life. Listen to opinions of well-meaning friends and family but always make the final choice yourself.